Entrepreneur
MAGAZINE'S

ULTIMATE

GUIDE TO

GOOGLE
AdWords

Entrepreneur
MAGAZINE'S

ULTIMATE

GUIDE TO

GOOGLE AdWords

FREE
*GOOGLE
SUCCESS
TOOLKIT*

AN $85.00 VALUE
Details inside

*How To Access 100 Million People
in 10 Minutes*

PERRY MARSHALL AND BRYAN TODD

EP
Entrepreneur.
Press

Editorial director: Jere L. Calmes
Cover design: Beth Hansen-Winter
Composition and production: Eliot House Productions

This publication is designed to provide accurate and authoritative information in regard to the
subject matter covered. It is sold with the understanding that the publisher is not engaged in ren-
dering legal, accounting, or other professional services. If legal advice or other expert assistance is
required, the services of a competent professional person should be sought.

Library of Congress Cataloging-in-Publication Data
Marshall, Perry S.
    Ultimate guide to Google adwords advertising/by Perry Marshall and Bryan Todd.
    p. cm.
    ISBN 1-59918-030-8 (alk. paper)
    1. Internet advertising. 2. Google. 3. Web search engines. I. Todd, Bryan. II. Title.
HF6146.I58M36 2006
659.14'4—dc22   2006026782

Printed in Canada

11 10 09 08 07 06   10 9 8 7 6 5 4 3 2 1

Contents

CHAPTER 1

Force Prospects to Choose Your Site

Google can bring thousands of visitors to your web site 24 hours a day, 7 days a week, 365 days a year, whether you're taking a shower, eating breakfast, driving to work, picking up your kids at school, taking a phone call, sleeping, sitting on the pot, daydreaming, busting your butt to beat a deadline, chasing some customer, typing an e-mail message . . .

■ ■ ■

It can all happen on autopilot with 100 percent predictability like clock-work. Ten years ago, an impossible dream—today, a reality.

Just think of the lengths entrepreneurs, business owners, and salespeople go to just to get a company off the ground, just to get a sale. I could recount in agonizing detail the *years* of my life I spent pounding the phone, pounding the pavement, making cold calls, renting trade show booths, going to no-show appointments, booking meetings that were a total waste of time.

But not anymore. I don't go to them anymore; they come to me. It's been that way so long, I'm very much used to it now. They'll come to you too.

Getting new customers is a real grind for a lot of people. It's the number-one obstacle to starting a new business. But all that can be a thing of the past. Instead of you chasing customers, they can now come to you, all day and all night via Google Adwords.

History will show Google AdWords to be the most important development in advertising of this decade. Never before has it been possible to spend $5, open an account, and have brand new, precisely targeted customers coming to your web site within minutes.

There are a lot of things you might want from Google. Maybe you're adding an online component to your retail operation, giving you steadier cash flow and deeper discounts from your suppliers. Maybe payroll is going to get easier. Maybe your consulting business will be positioned better. Maybe you're already getting traffic, but free listings are too unreliable. Maybe you've been successful selling on eBay, and now you want to play with the big boys. Maybe you're a working mom, and you'll finally be able to come home.

If you're privy to the secrets of online marketing, all those opportunities will open up to you. You'll have fresh hot sales leads waiting for you in your e-mail box every morning when you sit down at your desk. You'll have customers buying from you, orders coming in 24/7/365. Instead of you chasing them, they come to you. Instead of trying to *guess* whether your next product launch will work, you can *know*.

Why is this even possible? Because in the last five years, the very direction of business itself has reversed. In the old days (remember the 1990s?), entrepreneurs and salespeople chased customers with phone calls, letters, and ads in the newspaper. Now customers chase businesses on the web.

Back then you had a list of prospects, and you tried to get them to buy. Now the buyers—millions of them—are trolling the web every second of the day, looking for businesses that can scratch their itch.

Ever heard Woody Allen's saying, "90 percent of success is showing up"? The phrase takes on a whole new meaning in the 21st century. If you just *show up* on Google and its search partners, when people type in the right phrase, a starving crowd will bust your doors down to eat at your restaurant. They'll fill every table and book the kitchen with orders. If they like the daily special and the dessert, they'll come back and eat again. There's a big feast going on, *if* you show up.

Here you'll discover the secrets of showing up. Not just somewhere, but at the right places at the right times in front of the right people. And if you're already advertising on Google, you'll learn how to cut your bid prices 20 percent, 50 percent, maybe even 70 percent or more.

This book is for

- online catalog and "mail order" marketers.
- local retail stores and service businesses.
- niche product marketers.
- home businesses run from a spare bedroom or basement office.
- authors, speakers, consultants, and publishers.
- business-to-business marketers collecting sales leads.
- nonprofits, churches, and charities.
- resellers, repair services, and parts suppliers.
- online communities and membership sites.

Google AdWords can help your business whether you're the provervial little old lady selling quilts in Eastern Kentucky or the multinational corporation. You don't have to be a geek to do this; many of the best online marketers are nontechnical people who succeed simply because they understand their customers.

A lot of these success stories are from "invisible entrepreneurs." By invisible, I mean that their next door neighbors have no idea what they do, and probably just assume they're unemployed or something. But they're running micro-empires from their spare bedroom. And they're in hundreds of industries, ranging from the mundane to the ridiculous to the outrageously specialized. Some of these guys and gals are making *serious cash.*

> Google gets searched more than 250 million times every day. Every one of them is typed in by a person who has an itch they want to scratch.
>
> Source: Stephen E. Arnold, *The Google Legacy,* (Infonortics, 2005).

Tens, even hundreds of thousands of dollars a month. And they're not in "sleazy" businesses, either.

In this book I'm going to show you exactly how they do it, how to make sure they find you and buy from you, not someone else.

Got a watch with a second hand?

Tick.   3,000 people just searched Google for something and went to some-body's web site.

Tick.   3,000 more.

Tick.   3,000 more.

180,000 people a minute.

Every minute, all day long.

All night long.

Here they come. Every second. Every minute. Every hour.

Are they finding your web site? Are they buying from you? Or are they finding someone *else's* web site and buying from them instead?

They could be finding you. They *should* be finding you. They *can* find you and buy from you. Many of them will come to your site, buy from you, and come back again and again, *if* you follow the simple instructions in this book.

Google AdWords can be the traffic monster that feeds your autopilot market-ing machine and churns out a profit for you every day and every night, hitting the entire world up for customers while you sleep. Not just bringing you tire kickers but highly qualified buyers who are proactively looking for exactly what you sell right this very minute.

Buying from *you*. Not somebody else.

If the internet matters to your business, then no book you've ever bought has more potential to make or save you money than this one.

This book is written so you can blow through it fast and immediately launch your course to make serious money with Google insider marketing tactics. That's the fun part: Quickly implementing killer tactics that will flood your business with prospects and profit.

But there's a serious side, too. I've held nothing back here. So not only will you know how to play the Google AdWords game, you'll discover how to craft power-ful marketing messages and hooks, bond with your customers, and dominate your market.

In this book you'll discover:

- How to avoid tragic, costly mistakes that almost all Google advertisers and online entrepreneurs make, sometimes with techniques Google itself should teach you but doesn't.
- How to disaster-proof business start-ups and product launches, and pound the risk out of new ventures. (Since most times you've only got one or two shots to nail it, why would you want to leave anything to chance?)
- Profiles of successful online businesses. Having coached hundreds of online entrepreneurs to success, I've accumulated a list of vital characteristics that separate winners from losers—many of which defy normal business school wisdom.
- How to create ultra-persuasive Google ads and web pages that not only convert visitors to buyers, but automatically improve with time, making it impossible for your rivals to catch up to you.
- The advanced (but simple) shortcut secrets of getting deep into your customer's head, so you know exactly where his hot buttons are and how to punch them at will. Result: Customer loyalty that reaches fanatical levels, and a rabid customer base that eagerly buys almost everything you ask them to buy.

And if you're already advertising on Google, you'll get 30 percent to 300 percent more visitors, for less money than you're paying right now.

While many hard-core "let's get after it" types will mark up and dog ear this book, you can really start seeing results *while* you're reading it. There are shortcuts you can complete tonight, and see results before you go to bed an hour later. Your business can literally be better by tomorrow morning.

So strap on your crash helmet because you're in for a wild ride. *Onward!* Stick with me and my partner, Bryan, as we show you the secrets to online business success.

I've created an online supplement to this book with more than $85 worth of extended book chapters, audio interviews, information on specialized topics, and ongoing updates on Google's ever-changing rules. You can access it at www.perry marshall.com/supplement.

Here are some cool success stories I've gotten from my customers:

I was getting about 2,830 clicks per month with Google AdWords at $1.06 per click. I've spent about 8 hours total reading your stuff and implementing it. Based on the results of my last few days, I am on track to get 7,815 clicks in the next month and spend the same $3,000 a month … a savings of $23,400 per year, or $2,925 per hour for the eight hours I have invested. This is without doubt one of the absolute best investments I've ever made and I haven't even started! And yes, I have done most of this while sitting at home in my underwear.

—KEITH LEE, TMS, KENT, WA

I'm telling everyone that your book is "required reading" if they want to market online. I actually read your Definitive Guide *in one day, and that evening started my first AdWords campaign. I now have four of them running, and the average click-through rate for all campaigns is above 2 percent. I also get well over a 3 percent CTR (some as high as 15 percent) on my more targeted keywords. This has increased the traffic to my sites tenfold in some cases, and has made my monthly revenues much more consistent (which is always nice). Best of all, I've never had a keyword shut down by Google for low CTR, and I've only done one round of "peel and stick" with my ads. I give all the credit to my recent AdWords success to you and your book.*

—RYAN DEISS, THE GREAT EZINE EXPERIMENT, AUSTIN, TX

I finished my first ad campaign this past weekend and implemented it late Sunday evening using information primarily from you. The only other source I used was Google's FAQ. By Wednesday, all my keywords were strong or moderate with a 0.9 percent Click Thru Rate. My web page logs counted 34 visitors to my site from Google's AdWords campaign and I had the first sale on my page for a 3 percent conversion rate. Not great, but not bad either for a "very first timer" without all the bumps and bruises! Brand new customers for mere cents!

—REX A. HUDSON, WORLDWIDE INFORMATION SUPPLY ENTERPRISES LLC, CLOVER, SC

Since your last coaching call, we made the keyword matching changes as you recommended, and have the following to show you. Our overall CTR is 4.4 percent—our best ad is 12.4 percent, and the worst one is a very respectable 3.1 percent!

—SIMON CHEN, THE EIGHTBLACK GROUP,
MELBOURNE, AUSTRALIA

In two months have cut my Google advertising in half with five times the results. I now realize that a lead is a lead and I do not have to spend 50 cents for the same lead that now costs me 7 cents! Thanks for all of your help.

—BOB GOLDSTEIN, MR. CHECKOUT DISTRIBUTORS INC.,
BOCA RATON, FL

I took my click-thru rate from 0.9 percent to 5.7 percent after listening to your MP3 session. And our site just jumped from a Google Page Rank 2 to a Page Rank 6 yesterday, after the last Google dance.

—TONY KARA, MENDAX MICROSYSTEMS,
MONTREAL, QUEBEC

I was only about 30 pages in . . . but you did write: "Now Just DO it! You can have this up in ten minutes . . ." So I put up some new ads for my site. Within 30 minutes I got an order for $67.47. Since then, I've built my list into the thousands of subscribers in less than three months!

—KEN ALSTON, WWW.JAPANESE-MAPLE.COM,
EARLYSVILLE, VA

It's simply amazing watching my click-thru rate go from 0.3 percent up to 48.0 percent in less than 30 minutes. The most important part is, I AM BEATING THE COMPETITION in cost and, better yet, finding areas of "no competition." Thanks for such awesome marketing advice; your material is by far the most valuable I have purchased. Your concepts are working for me, and I intend on running this as a service for a lot of my web hosting clientele.

—JOHN FINNEY, HOST4NET AFFORDABLE
WEB SITE DESIGN AND HOSTING

WOW! I got a 500 percent increase in response . . . with just a quick "Band-Aid" fix. Can't wait to see what happens when I follow all of your suggestions.

—JENNY HAMBY, COPYWRITER & SEMINAR MARKETING CONSULTANT, SEMINARMARKETINGPRO.COM, PLAINFIELD, IL

Build Your
Own Autopilot
Marketing Machine

W e're not going to just teach you a handful of Google tricks.
We're going to show you how to make the internet your slave.
Plus you'll find out why selling on the internet is way simpler than most
people think, because only a handful of things really matter anyway.

■ ■ ■

If you're at a party and tell folks you're starting an online business, they
won't spare a bit of advice. They'll give you an endless list of things they
think you need: Flash animations, dedicated servers, shopping cart
scripts, META tags, secure authentication, pop-up windows, blogs,

domain name registrars, SQL servers, cascading style sheets, ASP—all kinds of stuff.

Are your eyes glazing over yet?

Some of the things on that list will certainly come into play for you at some point. But people way smarter than you or me have blown hundreds of thousands of dollars before the first visitor even showed up and bought anything. Big mistake.

Techno-wizardry is, for the most part, a distraction and a waste of time. So in this short chapter, we're going to show you the moving parts you need and just how simple a thriving, profitable web site can be.

IT ALL STARTS WHEN PEOPLE SEARCH FOR SOMETHING

Suzie types in "facial wrinkles" at her computer, and here's what shows up on Google:

On the top and right are the AdWords ads, which are paid. Running down the left are the free "organic" search listings.

She clicks on the ad on the right that says:

Your Wrinkles Disappear
Oprah, Melanie, Goldie, Demi, Nora,
Beyonce, Marisa and Dr. Weil agree
CelebrityBeautySecret.com

Or Suzy is trolling the web and she's at www.PriceGrabber.com reading reviews of *The Complete Idiot's Guide to Cosmetic Surgery*:

And she sees the ad at the very bottom that says

No More Cosmetic Surgery

Erase Your Wrinkles in Minutes As Seen on
Oprah, ABC & Vogue
CelebrityBeautySecret.com

This ad is also served by Google through the *AdSense* program to dozens, hundreds, possibly thousands of web sites.

The ad sounds interesting. She clicks on the ad, and she's taken to this page:

That's the first step. Now there are only three things that can happen: Suzy can buy, she can ask for more information, or she can leave.

For a lot of sites, the best thing to offer is information instead of offering a product up front. The way Suzy gets it is by entering her address to get a gift, sample, download, white paper, report, or guide. This is especially important if the problem Suzy wants to solve is an ongoing area of interest, as opposed to a one-time impulse buy.

If this was a product for people with diabetes, for example, it would be a very good idea to collect Suzy's e-mail address, because if Suzy is a diabetic, she's going to have diabetes next week and next year, not just today. Many Suzies could be a valuable e-mail list! Plus this gives you a chance to talk to all the Suzies on your list and get to know them better.

So, again, when she comes to your site, there are only three things that can happen:

1. Suzy buys the skin cream.
2. Suzy leaves.
3. Suzy asks for information and can come back later—because you've got her e-mail address.

You do need to get her e-mail address, and invite her to come back and try another product. That's the process. That's what this is all about. *Anything that gets this done is good. Anything that complicates it or gets in the way is bad.*

See, this is really simple. Futzing around with Flash presentations and 19 different ways to build a web page, all that stuff is beside the point. The point is: *Scratch Suzy's itch and move the stuff from your shelf to hers, as quickly, easily, and simply as possible.*

YOUR MISSION, SHOULD YOU CHOOSE TO ACCEPT IT

Your mission is to buy clicks for $1 and make $2 while Suzy is on your web site. Your mission is to make more money from your clicks than your competitors make from theirs. That's it.

Most people don't realize how powerful this concept is—and why Google AdWords is usually the best place to make this happen. The rest of this book is all about how to do this.

IF YOU DO THIS RIGHT, IT CAN MAKE YOU RICH

My friend and legendary marketer Jonathan Mizel says, "Internet traffic goes where it's rewarded, respected, and paid for." If you reward and respect your visitors, and if you're able to pay more for them than everyone else advertising in your category, *then you can have as much traffic as you want.* The traffic will literally *seek you out.*

This is not an exaggeration. It's completely true. But traffic will only seek you out when it's profitable.

So you develop your Google campaigns, send traffic to your site, collect information requests, make sales, follow up with your customers, and do whatever you need to do to make the whole process flow like water running downhill.

Then, and only then, do you go to all of the *other* traffic sources available to you, like Yahoo/Overture, banner ads, e-mail lists, and affiliates. As we'll discuss in other chapters, these are useful additions. Affiliates (people who send you traffic in exchange for commission on sales) can be a *huge* source of traffic. If your web site doesn't pay, affiliates won't send you anything. But good affiliates will turn the tide in your favor, making you the dominant force in your market.

A FEW TOOLS THAT WILL HELP YOU GET STARTED

Whether you're selling skin cream, e-books, computer games, or imported wood carvings, you need a handful of things to be in business:

- A domain name
- A web site with web pages
- An e-mail broadcast / auto responder service
- A shopping cart service
- A product to sell
- A Google AdWords account

The online supplement to this book (www.perrymarshall.com/supplement) has links to dozens of resources for getting these things done, plus additional tutorials and MP3 files. Here's a quick rundown of the most important stuff.

- You can register a domain name at www.GoDaddy.com. You can also host your web site there.

- You don't need a fancy web site, and Jim Edwards has a terrific system for building simple web sites at www.MiniWebCreator.com.
- You can create your web pages with Microsoft Front Page® or Macromedia Dreamweaver.®
- An excellent e-mail system is www.AweberSystem.com. You can queue up automatic messages that go out when people request information or buy. You can send e-mail newsletters and announcements to your customers and prospects. AweberSystem also does a good job of getting your messages through the spam filters.
- If you're just getting started, *do not* futz around with installing software on your server, etc. Go to a third party like www.1ShoppingCartSystem.com, which has a great service that allows you to quickly set up order forms, take orders, process credit card transactions, follow up with e-mails, and manage your customer list.
- The product is up to you, but even if you don't have one yet, you can be an affiliate for someone else's product and sell theirs. It's a great way to get your feet wet because you're not committed to anything long term. You can use your Google ads and your web site to learn about any market you want and decide if you want to stay in it.

You can find thousands of affiliate products and programs at www.Click Bank.com and www.CJ.com, and you may use these sites to sell your own digital product. These sites process orders for you, handle refunds and basic customer service problems, and pay affiliates.

Chapter 3 shows you how to quickly set up a Google account.

THE NEW GOLDEN AGE OF ENTREPRENEURSHIP

Years ago if you wanted to start a direct marketing business, not only did you have to have a product and get set up to fulfill it, you had to depend on a bunch of other people and complex procedures just to sell the very first unit. You had to rent mailing lists, hire printers to print letters, send out the letters, place ads in magazines—and then *wait*. Weeks or months usually, a few days at the absolute minimum. The process was very cumbersome.

Now you can use third-party tools like the ones I described, stick up a web site, open a Google account, and have traffic coming to your site in ten minutes.

Literally ten minutes. If the project fails, you scrap it and try a different one. If the market stinks, you go find a new one. If your project succeeds, it can grow faster than ever before in the history of the world.

Let's get this Google account started, shall we?

Build a Google Campaign from Scratch— the Right Way

There's nothing more frustrating than building a web site and waiting for people to just "show up." It's worse than watching paint dry. That's why Pay Per Click marketing is a miracle of the modern world. Never before has it been possible to spend $5, open an account, and have brand new, precisely targeted customers coming to your web site within minutes.

■ ■ ■

Ten minutes from right now you can have a Google campaign up and running, sending visitors to your web site. The speed at which you can do new things and make changes in Google's system is stunning.

But speed can also be a trap. Sometimes people do rash things when they're in a hurry.

This is a short chapter, but it contains some seriously important concepts. Take a little time and go through these steps and it'll save you a lot of money. And you'll still have your Google campaign up and running in an hour or two—and it'll be set up better than 95 percent of the other Google campaigns on the net.

THREE QUESTIONS THAT TELL WHETHER A MARKET IS FOR YOU

It's really easy to blow money on Pay Per Click—you can pick a keyword, write an ad, and get a bunch of visitors who cost you money but have no chance of ever wanting to buy something from you. The following questions will help make sure you don't buy the wrong kind of traffic for your web site.

Ask this first:

1. How Many People Are Looking for this Product?

Your answer will keep your expectations realistic and prevent you from running into disappointment later if you discover that Google can't bring you as many new customers as you had hoped. Even if that happens, odds are you'll discover other untapped traffic sources that are less competitive but every bit as profitable.

You can get a quick estimate in a matter of seconds. Overture has a helpful search-term suggestion tool at http://inventory.overture.com (or http://inventory.uk.overture.com for the U.K.). Enter a handful of your main general keywords, and Overture will tell you how many searches its servers got last month for each one.

In the last chapter you saw some ads and web pages for Julie Brumlik's company, Dremu Skincare, which sells a skin-care product designed to slow the aging process. Let's imagine she's just getting started and wants to bring more folks to her web site through Google. Where does she start?

The first thing to do is to brainstorm a starter list of possible keywords. She's got plenty to work from:

skin
beauty
acne
cosmetics
makeup
cosmetic surgery
dermatology
anti-aging
wrinkles
oils
moisturizers

And this is nowhere near complete. But if we run over to Overture's keyword selector tool and enter these terms to see how many searches they get in a month, here's what we find out:

skin	7,290
beauty	5,006
acne	1,872
cosmetics	1,862
makeup	1,796
cosmetic surgery	1,736
dermatology	622
anti-aging	503
wrinkles	485
oils	390
moisturizers	120

Notice what's going on here:

- The keyword "skin" got over *60 times* as many searches as the bottom term, "moisturizers." That term may be one of your most valuable players.
- When you run your Overture inventory search on any one of these keywords, you'll invariably get a list of irrelevant terms as well. Those will become your *negative keywords*. More on that in Chapter 4.
- There's a huge number of people who may want skin-care products but who'll use different word combinations than are on the lists we've come up

with. So we'll need to brainstorm for more, and then search Overture's tool again.

According to Overture, we could conceivably get tens, even hundreds of thousands of U.S. searches in a month on those top keywords. But those clicks aren't free.

2. How Much Will Your Clicks Cost?

Do you want to know what it would cost to run your ad at the top of the page? Google will tell you. It'll also give you a rougher estimate of what your costs and ad position will be if you want to bid a lower price.

To get the price for that top position, click on the option "Want to purchase the most clicks possible?"

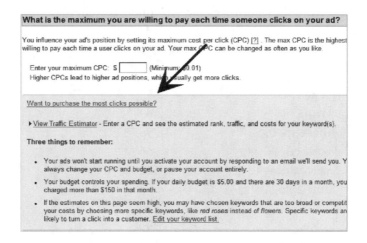

Just below that, Google's Traffic Estimator tells you the estimated rank, traffic, and costs for your keywords. We'll show you a working example of this later when we walk you through the setup process.

But how do you know what to pay for your clicks? That's a judgment call that you'll need to make, based on your particular market, the keywords you've picked, the initial budget that you're on, and your ability to turn visitors into buyers. The simple answer, though, is *visitor value*. It's the average amount that each visitor spends with you. It's the secret to knowing what bid prices can be, and it's the secret to attracting affiliates, too. More on visitor value in Chapter 17.

3. Who Are Your Competitors?

Google displays their paid ads on the right hand side of the page, and in the top two or three positions on the upper left. To find out how many advertisers there are, take note of the topmost ad and then go through each subsequent search page until you see that ad repeat. The total number of ads you see before the top one is repeated is the number of advertisers who are currently bidding on that keyword.

Or you can set your Google preferences to 100 results per page. To find this setting, click on the "preferences" link next to the search box. That way you'll see all of your competitors in one place.

The more bidders there are, the tougher it's going to be for you to stay in the market and make a profit. In our opinion, less than 15 bidders means it's going to be comparatively easy for you. More than 50 means that the market is going to be nasty, and you'll need to use every trick in the book in order to stay competitive.

There's nothing wrong with going into a hypercompetitive market. The more competitors there are, the more money is available to the winners. So if you test your ads, put up persuasive descriptions of your products, use e-mail to follow up, and watch your numbers, you can win in literally any market. Just remember that the more bidders there are, the more money you will have to invest in testing before you'll become profitable.

Google normally displays 8 to 11 ads per page, so if you want to be guaranteed to show up on the first page of search results (which you virtually always do), then you need to aim for position 8 or better and set your maximum cost-per-click high enough to stay there.

SET UP YOUR CAMPAIGN

To start your campaign, go to https://adwords.google.com, and find the "Click to begin" button:

We'll show you how to set up an account using Google's "standard edition" setup method:

1. Choose your language and location

Choose the language(s) that you want to reach.

Next, decide how large or small a geographic area you want to target. You can choose whole countries, regions of countries, states or provinces, or cities. You can also choose custom-designated geographic areas, such as latitude-longitude coordinates or the radius of a set number of miles or kilometers around a specific address.

Select the country or countries where you want your ads to show.

2. Write Your First Ad

We'll enter the "CRM Software" ad that we've written:

Create an ad

Example short ad:

CRM Software
1-to-1 Marketing for Every Prospect
30-Day Free Trial & 24/7 Support
www.CRM1to1.com/FreeTrial

Headline:	CRM Software	Max 25 characters
Description line 1:	1-to-1 Marketing for Every Prospect	Max 35 characters
Description line 2:	30-Day Free Trial & 24/7 Support	Max 35 characters
Display URL: [?]	http:// www.CRM1to1.com/FreeTrial	Max 35 characters
Destination URL: [?]	http:// ▾ www.CRM1to1.com/FreeTrial	Max 1024 characters

< Back   Reset Ad   Continue »

Now let's explain what we just did, and why.

More people click on ads when the *headline* includes the keyword they're searching on. So use your keywords in your headline when you can. You're limited to 25 characters, so for some search terms you'll need to use abbreviations or shorter synonyms.

The *second and third lines* allow for 35 characters of text each. In most markets, you'll be more successful if you describe a *benefit* on the second line, followed by a *feature* or *offer* on the third line. Later on, you can test which order works.

The *fourth line* is your *display URL,* which is the web address that people will see in your ad. The URL you show has to resolve to an actual location on your site, though it doesn't necessarily have to be the specific landing page that you take people to.

The last line is your actual *destination URL,* or your landing page. You can use a tracking link for this, or a link that takes people to your chosen page.

If you want to irritate your customer, send him to your home page hoping he'll just look around. (Everyone loves to troll around somebody's site for ten minutes looking for something that should be obvious but isn't—right?) But if you actually want him to sign up or buy from you, take him to a specific page that's tailor-made for his specific search.

Want more clicks? You should always test a second ad against this one and find a winner. Google will let you enter that ad after you've finished setting up your account.

3. Insert Your Keywords

Paste your keywords. We'll start with just two, and we'll put both of them in brackets [ ] to be sure that the only searches we get initially are for those exact words typed in by themselves.

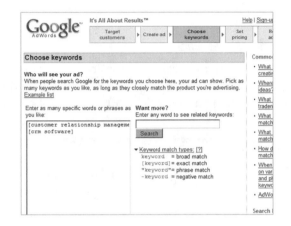

Note: When you're getting started, it's *not* a good idea to dump hundreds or thousands of keywords in. Start with a few important ones and work from there.

4. Choose Your Currency and Set Your Daily Ad Budget

If for example, you can only afford $50 per day instead of $170, it's better to control your spending by cutting your bid prices than by only cutting your daily budget. This is because the daily budget tool causes your ads to be served for only part of the day, rather than a full 24 hours.

Lower positions convert to sales better, generally. So if you're on a limited budget, it's better to just go to the last position on the page and be seen all the time than to be at the top, cut your daily budget, and be seen only one-fourth of the time.

Note: Set your daily budget such that if you screw up big time, your checking account won't be emptied out. You can always come back and bump it up, but it's always nice to have a safety net.

5. Set Your Maximum Cost-Per-Click

Set your maximum price now, but realize that every keyword is theoretically a different market, which means that each major one will need a bid price of its own. Google will let you set individual bids for each keyword later.

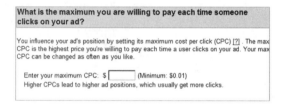

If you click on the "Want to purchase the most possible clicks?" link, Google will show you the top current bid for all of your keywords. Bidding at this price (which is often terribly expensive and may draw excessive clicks from marginally interested tire-kickers) will guarantee that your ads show up in top position for these keywords.

Google also gives you a rough estimate of your traffic, your cost, and your average position. Most of the time, though, those estimates are inaccurate. Don't bet your life on them.

6. Review Everything

Double check your ad, your keywords, your cost-per-click, and your daily budget to be sure you start your campaign off the right way.

7. Enter Your E-Mail Address and Password

Google will send you an e-mail with a special URL that you can click through or enter into your browser to confirm that your login information is valid.

8. Enter Your Billing Information

Your ads will start showing as soon as you confirm your payment information. Now you're set.

THINGS YOU CAN TWEAK NOW

You can almost always improve on the number of clicks you'll get from the ad you've just written. As you'll see later, it's almost impossible to guess what is going to make people click; you need to let the visitors vote. So write a second ad you think can beat it, and go back into your ad group to post it:

Google will rotate this automatically against your first ad, and after a few days or weeks, you can pick the winner and delete the loser. Results will come in faster if you test just two at a time.

You can also add more keywords to your list, adjust your cost-per-click or destination URL for individual keywords, create more ad groups and campaigns, and adjust your campaign settings to fit your style.

In Chapter 25, we'll look at the bells and whistles that Google gives you for managing and tweaking your campaigns, and we'll give you some cool tips for getting more clicks and sales from your ads through smarter traffic management.

When you follow these steps, a campaign will grow that is unique to you and your customers. The success is yours, and so is the profit. It's your business, unlike any other, with your fingerprints and personality all over it. Yours alone. Nobody can replicate that.

THE MAGIC IS IN THE PROCESS

The most important thing you could possibly know about a Google campaign is that it's not a single technique or something that you set up once and forget about.

Now we do have clients who've barely touched their Google campaigns in two years, and they're pumping the visitors through every day. However, the real power in Google AdWords is the fact that by logging in every few days or once a week you can make constant refinements and increase your traffic two, five, or ten times. The number of visitors grows even while your cost-per-click declines over time.

These refinements don't take a lot of time—sometimes only a few *minutes* each month. But you earn compound interest on those efforts because your profit margins get fatter as the traffic grows.

SET YOURSELF UP FOR SUCCESS

Already you know how to build a small, basic ad campaign. Now the foundation for future success is laid by organizing larger groups and campaigns properly. In the next chapter, you'll learn how to do that.

Meet Uncle Claude

If You've Ever Sold Anything on the Internet, This Man Is Your Uncle

Every field of knowledge exists because a handful of luminaries made ground-breaking discoveries and showed others the way. And there's almost always one who stands head and shoulders above the others.

In management, it's Peter Drucker. In engineering, it's Thomas Edison. In physics, Albert Einstein. In Rock & Roll, it's the Beatles. For saxophone players, it's John Coltrane. In results-driven advertising, it's Claude Hopkins, who lived from 1866–1932. Whether you know it or not, if your web site is generating a profit, it's because you've discovered something that Hopkins probably figured out, before the turn of the last century.

Uncle Claude invented the coupon (which he created so advertisers could track their results) and pioneered concepts like split testing, premiums, free samples, and mail-order marketing. In fact, his book *Scientific Advertising* is so important we've included it in the online supplement to this book at www.perrymarshall.com/supplement.

In the rest of this book, we take Hopkins' ideas, which in the late 1800s took months to implement and test, and show you how to do the same thing, literally *10,000 times faster.* We've included choice nuggets of wisdom from him in many of the upcoming chapters.

So consider him your advice-giving Uncle Claude. Thanks to Uncle Claude, it's never been easier, or more *scientific,* to make a fortune in marketing.

CHAPTER 4

Pay Less and Get More Clicks

Most mistakes people make in their Google campaigns are pretty common, and 90 percent of Google campaigns can be greatly improved with less than an hour of effort. You can save yourself hundreds, thousands, even tens of thousands of dollars in the hour you spend following our instructions.

■ ■ ■

We do a *lot* of Google AdWords consultations, both through our coaching programs and our web site where people come to look for help. We get on the phone with our customer, and the two of us log into the Google account to see what can be improved. It's not unusual to improve performance by 50 percent or 100 percent in as little as 30 minutes.

Want to know what the number-one mistake people make is? *Improperly organized campaigns.* Badly organized ads and keywords cripple your Google campaigns and cost you a *ton* of money. Properly organized campaigns get results from the beginning and are easy to adjust and optimize. Over time this makes a huge difference.

In a *perfect* world, you'd serve up a perfect ad for every single keyword someone types in. Since each keyword is different, each ad would be different, too. If you had 2,000 keywords, then you'd have to write 2,000 ads, too.

In the real world, that's kind of impractical. So you cluster similar keywords together with a single ad. *Ad groups* are the smallest individual units that contain your keywords and your ads together. You can have multiple ad groups in a single campaign. A *campaign* is just a handy way to organize ad groups, usually according to broad topic.

In a single Google account, you can have as many campaigns as you want. Some of the campaigns in your account may be on a completely different topic, selling completely different services, and sending traffic to a completely different web site.

How you separate your *campaigns* is up to you. How you separate *ad groups,* however, is one of those areas where there's a right way and a wrong way.

THE WRONG WAY TO ORGANIZE AN ADWORDS CAMPAIGN

Most beginners set up their campaigns to look something like this:

Smith Telecommunications
Robust Solutions for
All Your Voice Mail Needs
www.smithtelecom.com

auto attendant
business telephone systems
call management systems
voice mail
voice mail equipment

voice mail service
voice mail systems

Then they send all the visitors to the home page, which has a bunch of different links to "Services," "Equipment," "Q&A," "About Us," "Contact Us," etc.

So if we made a map of their AdWords campaign, it would look like:

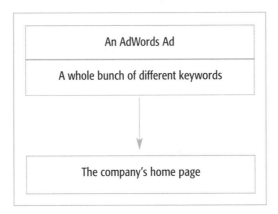

What's wrong with this picture? It's destined to fail. Here's why:

- There are too many different kinds of keywords in the same group. Every one of these keywords needs to be in its own group, along with a list of very similar words and phrases.
- The ad doesn't match the keywords, and it can't, because there are too many different kinds of keywords in the group.
- "Smith Telecommunications," or the name of almost any business, is a *lousy* headline. The clickthrough rate (CTR) is going to be very low, and therefore the bid prices will be higher.
- The ad is about Smith Telecommunications, not what the customer really wants. Your ads need to be about your customer, not about yourself!
- A person who searches for "voice mail service" needs to be taken to a page about voice mail service; a person who searches for equipment needs to be taken to a *different* web page about voice mail equipment. These are two entirely different topics. If a person has to figure out where to go after they land on your web page, you're making them work too hard. You need to show them exactly what they were searching for.

If you structure your campaigns properly from the beginning, it's a *lot* easier to make this work. Here's how you organize your ads and keywords:

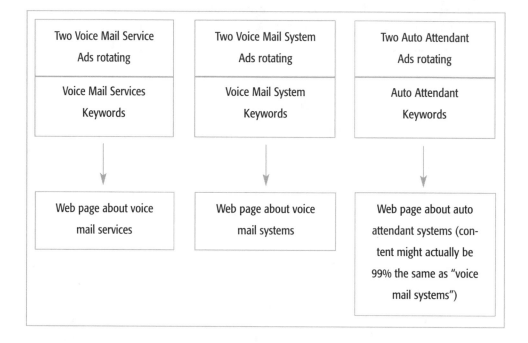

To do this, take all of your different keywords and use Wordtracker (www.wordtracker.info) or Overture (http://inventory.overture.com) to organize them into narrow "silos" of very tightly related terms. They will look like this:

Voice Mail Services	**Voice Mail System**	**Auto Attendant**
voice mail provider	voice mail systems	answering attendant auto system
voice mail service	voice mail systems for realtors	auto attendant voice mail services
voice mail service provider	telemarketing and voice mail systems	auto attendant
voice mail services	phone systems voice mail	auto attendant phone system
	home office voice mail systems	auto attendant software
	home office telephone voice mail systems	auto attendant system
		auto attendant voice mail
		phone auto attendant

There's another step we need to take before pasting this into a campaign: Consider negative keywords. Here's a list of keywords that come from "Voice Mail Software."

> voice mail software
> voice mail business software
> voice mail software for panasonic
> voice mail broadcasting software
> voice mail business software
> multiple voice mail software
> mac voice mail software
> multi-line voice mail system software vru
> norstar voice mail software
> software to record voice mail
> free voice mail software

You might not want visitors who want something for *free*. Your company also has nothing to do with voice *broadcasting* and you don't have anything for *MacIntosh* computers. So turn those into negative keywords by putting a minus sign in front of them. The above list now looks like this:

> voice mail software
> voice mail business software
> voice mail software for panasonic
> voice mail business software
> multiple voice mail software
> multi-line voice mail system software vru
> norstar voice mail software
> software to record voice mail
>
> –free
> –mac
> –macintosh   Negative Keywords
> –broadcast
> –broadcasting

So when you set up your ad campaigns, each one of these keyword lists is going to go into a different group with its own set of ads.

SPLIT-TEST YOUR ADS!

We'll write two ads. Google will rotate them simultaneously. One will have a better CTR than the other. We'll later delete the inferior one, write a new one, and try again. Little by little your CTR will go up, up, up.

Tip: The key to long-term success on AdWords—and keeping your bid prices down—is always split testing two ads at the same time, then deleting the inferior one and trying to beat the best one. Always have two ads running at the same time.

> ## Voice Mail Software
> Make Your Communication Easier
> With Custom, Expandable Systems
> www.SmithTelecom.com/VMsoftware

- ↤ Headline contains your keywords
- ↤ 2nd line contains a BENEFIT
- ↤ 3rd line contains a FEATURE or OFFER
- ↤ 4th line: Display URL has a keyword in the subdirectory /VMsoftware that will help the CTR

> ## Voice Mail Software
> For Any Business & Any Phone System
> Same Day Installation & Easy Terms
> www.SmithTelecom.com/VMsoftware

Same formula for Ad#2, but we're testing a different message. Notice that we capitalize the important words, that usually helps.

So here's what we've done:

- We've generated a list of various keywords: Voice mail system, voice mail software, voice mail service, auto attendant, etc.
- We've used keyword research tools to drill down and generate many variations on these keywords.
- Each family of keywords goes into its own group.
- We rotate two ads at the same time, all the time, and constantly try to beat our best.
- When visitors click on the ad, they are taken to the exact page on your site that has a specific solution to their exact problem, not the home page. No guessing or clicking all over the place to find what they want.

Here's another example of how to cluster keywords into groups and campaigns, for a variety of martial arts related terms:

Organize Your Campaigns and Ad Groups					
	Campaign #1 Self Defense	Campaign #2 Martial Arts	Campaign #3 Fighting	Campaign #4 Security & Safety	Campaign #5 Protection
Ad Group #1	Women's Self Defense	Karate	Wrestling	Personal Safety	Self Protection
Ad Group #2	Defense Class	Tae Kwon Do	Grappling	Women's Safety	Women's Protection
Ad Group #3	Defense Video	Aikido	Hand-to-Hand Combat	Personal Security	Child Protection
Ad Group #4	Defense Tactic	Hapkido	Weapons Combat	Children's Security	Assault protection

Do you want to make it easy to manage campaigns and match your keywords well to ads within each ad group? Organize your campaigns this way, and they will be. More importantly, you'll get more clicks.

CUT OUT IRRELEVANT KEYWORDS TO IMPROVE YOUR CTR

Sometimes in your keyword collecting you'll inadvertently be bidding on terms in your keyword list that don't belong at all. For example:

☐ [religion during the renaissance]		0
☐ [ancient greece religion]		0
☐ "hindu religion"		0
☐ "ancient egypt religion"		0
☐ "losing my religion lyrics"		0
☐ [asian religions]		0
☐ [mesopotamia religion]		0

Most of the keywords here, in fact, are irrelevant to what we were going after. They got zero clicks. Of course, the "losing my religion lyrics" search term takes the cake. We'll delete that keyword and then stick in the term "lyrics" as a negative keyword. We'll get a higher CTR, since now that big fat "0" is no longer bringing down the average.

THE PEEL AND STICK STRATEGY: GET A HIGHER
CTR BY MOVING YOUR KEYWORDS AROUND

Look at this example of an ad group with keywords that are getting a great CTR.
Notice how some of these keywords could be headlines of their own:

Organized Religion - 2005	+ Create New Text Ad | Image Ad				
7 Great Lies Of Organized Religion A Hard Look at Past & Present CoffeehouseTheology.com	1 of 2 Ads: View all below				
Delete Edit CPCs/URLs					
☐ Keyword	Status [?]	Max CPC Bid	Clicks ▼	Impr.	CTR A
Search Total			189	3,753	5.0%
Content Total [?]			0	2,094	0.0%
☐ "organized religion"	Active		145	2,885	5.0%
☐ [organized religion]	Active		29	542	5.3%
☐ organized religion	Active		15	326	4.6%

We noticed that. So we did something about it. We pulled those keywords out
of that list and came up with several brand new ad groups. Here's one:

Dark History of Religion	+ Create New Text Ad | Image Ad				
7 Great Lies Of Organized Religion A Hard Look at Past & Present CoffeehouseTheology.com	7,878 Clicks | 0.3% CTR | Served - 100.0% [more info] Edit - Delete				
Delete Edit CPCs/URLs					
☐ Keyword	Status [?]	Max CPC Bid	Clicks ▼	Impr.	CTR
Search Total			271	10,484	2.5%
Content Total [?]			7,607	2,295,102	0.3%
☐ history of religion	Active		150	6,431	2.3%
☐ [history of religion]	Active		100	3,314	3.0%

The CTR on [history of religion] jumped from 2.2 percent up to 3.0 percent.
That's *an improvement of 36 percent,* with so little work!

But it gets better:

Religion Run Amok	+ Create New Text Ad	Image Ad
7 Great Lies Of Organized Religion	
A Hard Look at Past & Present	1 of 21 Ads: View all below
CoffeehouseTheology.com	

Delete   Edit CPCs/URLs

☐ Keyword	Status [?]	Max CPC Bid	Clicks ▼	Impr.	CT
Search Total			5,106	605,222	0.8
Content Total [?] — image ads			0	0	
Content Total [?] — text ads			1,843	1,270,376	0.1
☐ what is religion			501	19,380	2.5
☐ world religion			153	15,126	1.0
☐ [history of religion] ←			123	5,424	2.2
☐ jewish religion			107	2,017	5.3
☐ [freedom from religion]			91	2,700	3.3
☐ [anti religion]			86	2,713	3.1
☐ [what is religion]			79	6,291	1.2
☐ christian religion ←			77	7,787	0.9
☐ "catholic religion"			69	7,759	0.8
☐ world religions			67	4,778	1.4
☐ "organized religion" ←			65	2,316	2.8
☐ [world religion]			63	6,545	0.9

That improved the clickthrough rate by 79 percent! Impressive. Plus, you'll notice that the keyword shows up not once but twice in the ad copy. That didn't hurt one bit.

Want a better CTR? Want higher positions on the page without paying any more per click? Want more profit in your pocket at the end of the month? This trick will work for you again and again. It's called *Peel and Stick.* You take a high traffic keyword, *peel* it out of a group and *stick* it in a new one with its own ad. It only takes a few minutes.

Peel and Stick Is So Simple and Powerful

Sometimes after you turn on your traffic, you'll discover that there are keywords in your ad groups that get a lot more hits than you were expecting. *And* their CTRs, you're convinced, could be a lot higher.

Delete any keyword you find like that and stick it into a new ad group with a clever ad that matches it perfectly. That's Peel and Stick. As simple as that. This can do wonders for your CTRs. Why does this work so well? Very simply, it's because people are more likely to click on your ad if they see your keyword in the headline.

Want to improve your CTR by as much as 80 percent? Organize your keywords differently.

MORE EASY-TO-FOLLOW EXAMPLES

Below are some ads that some of our associates ran for their businesses, with a sample of a few of the actual keywords they used. Best part is, they're far from perfect. They can be improved even more.

How to Sell Anything
Skills Your Competitors Don't Have
Powerful Secrets You Won't Believe
www.XYZ.com

   how to sell
   [how to sell]
   "how to sell"
   –marijuana
   –devil
   –soul

These negative keywords are kind of funny. You definitely don't want those searches!

Dentures to Be Proud Of
Free In-Office Consultation & More
For a Smile that Wins New Friends
www.XYZ.com

   dentures
   affordable dentures
   denture repair
   same-day dentures
   permanent dentures
   partial denture

How many clicks is "denture repair" or "partial denture" getting? If there are a lot, each of them needs Peel and Stick.

Power Supplies to Order
Custom Design Requests Welcomed
Any OEM Application, ISO 9002
www.XYZ.com

   power supply
   power supplies
   12 volt power supply
   5v power supply
   class 2 power supply
   ac power supply

Try a separate ad group just for "AC power supply."

A/C Transformers Qty 250+
For OEM Applications, ISO 9002
Custom 1-Day Quote, Fast Delivery
www.XYZ.com

   transformers
   power transformer
   transformer accessories
   power supply transformers
   power transformer tube
   –robots in disguise

Admittedly, the length of some of these search terms might make Peel and stick a bit challenging, especially if you're trying to fit the keyword in the headline and be descriptive at the same time.

Toothache Relief, Finally!
Your Local Pain-Free Dentist
Improves Your Health & Much More
www.XYZ.com

    toothache
    toothaches
    toothache remedies
    toothache cure
    toothache relief
    toothache pain

If "toothache remedies" gets enough searches to make a difference, do Peel and Stick with it.

Day Trading Course
Develop Your Personal Schedule
Maximize Your Trading Potential
www.XYZ.com

    trading course
    [trading course]
    trading training
    [trading training]
    "trading books"
    commodities course
    futures course

If "trading training" is getting enough clicks already, pull it out and put it with a new ad. "Commodities course" and "futures course" belong in their own separate ad groups, no question.

If you organize your Google ad groups so that your keywords call out to searchers from your headline and ad text, you can get more visitors to your site, earn better positions on the page, and pay less money for your clicks.

Do you want to improve your clickthrough rate by 10 percent, 30 percent, 80 percent, or better, and not have to pay a penny more per click? It's all in how you organize things. As simple as this is—so simple that most people miss it the first time—it's the single most effective secret for you to get more clicks without paying a penny more.

Uncle Claude Sez

You are presenting an ad to millions. Among them is a percentage, small or large, whom you hope to interest. Go after that percentage and try to strike the chord that responds . . . They will decide by a glance—by your headline . . . . Address the people you seek and them only.

CHAPTER 5

Develop High-Quality Keyword Lists to Craft Killer Headlines

You'll capture the attention of your customer when you enter the conversation already taking place inside her head. With Google, you do this, and get more clicks as a result, by using your keywords skillfully in your ad. Bid on more keywords and you can capture the attention of more people.

■ ■ ■

At my house we've got a wonderful children's book called *No, David!* David is a little boy whose mom is constantly telling him, "No, David!"

David is about to knock over a potted plant.

"No, David!"

David is chewing with his mouth open.

"No, David!"

David is playing baseball in the living room.

"No, David!"

David is about to push the aquarium off the table and spill the goldfish out on the floor.

"No, David!"

From the first moment, my son Cuyler was *glued* to this book. For months it was his favorite book in the whole world.

Why?

You already know why.

It's because Cuyler's Mamma (and Daddy) were always shouting *"No, Cuyler!"* (Maybe it was because he was knocking over potted plants, chewing with his mouth open, playing baseball in the living room, and spilling the goldfish all over the floor.)

The only way to make it better would be to have a book called *No, Cuyler!* (Who knows? Maybe somebody will start selling personalized versions of the book.)

Cuyler had a favorite part of the story. Know what it was? It was at the very end, when David's mom says, "Come here, David." Mamma gives David a hug and says, "I love you, David." Cuyler *loved* that page. Especially the hug he got every time we closed the book.

Cuyler loved *No, David!* because this book described a day—every day—in the life of Cuyler. *No David!* is like a page from his own diary.

Nothing endears you to your customer like reading his own diary, showing that you know what it feels like to be *him*. Telling him exactly what his day was like today. And *that's* what it means to enter the conversation inside your customer's head. When you step right into his thoughts and talk to him the way he talks to other people and himself about things that are important to him, he'll listen to you. Just like Cuyler did.

The keyword people type in *is* the conversation inside their head, at that very moment. Your ad will capture peoples' interest when it repeats to them what they're thinking. So putting your keywords in your headline, *and* in the body of your ad, *and* in your URL are all part of a sound advertising strategy.

The more places in your ad that you have keywords showing up, the better your chances of getting the clicks. That means the headline. That might mean the body of the ad. That even means the display URL. If someone types in "German" or "Learn German," notice how many times they'll see their keyword in this ad:

Want to Learn German?

5 Crucial Principles You Must Know
To Master German, and Fast
www.MasterGermanFaster.com

If effective marketing means speaking directly to what people are searching on and repeating it back at them, how do you go about finding out what people are searching on in the first place? Where do you go to get the good keywords, especially the keywords that are worth the most money?

MORE TOOLS FOR YOUR TOOLBOX

The quickest place to start is with Overture's Keyword Selector Tool, available for free at http://inventory.overture.com. We've told you about this one already. It gives you an immediate sense of how valuable each of your keywords will be relative to the others.

458,579	learn german
103,157	german shepherd
85,210	german
22,970	german dictionary
16,990	german english dictionary
16,294	german translation
15,992	german shepherd dog
14,409	german translator
13,037	german shepherd puppy
11,646	english german dictionary
10,187	german to english
9,810	german to english translation
9,800	german short hair pointer

One look at this list and it's obvious where the traffic and money will be. It's also obvious that you've got keywords here that don't belong.

GET RID OF VISITORS YOU DON'T WANT

You haven't spent a penny yet and you already know what your major *negative keywords* are going to be. These are words you include in your list where you specifically do not want your ad to show when people type them in. You enter them into your keyword list with negatives in front of them. For example:

–dog

–puppy

–shepherd

–pointer

–dictionary

–translator

–translation

–hair

–etc.

Your ads won't show anytime people include these words in their search.

NOW THE MONEY CAN DO THE TALKING

So how much will these keywords actually cost to bid on? To get your answer, head over to the Yahoo Resource Center, which you can find at www.overture.com, and click to see the "Bids Tool." When you enter "learn German" in the pop-up search box, Overture gives you a list of the prices advertisers are paying to promote their products on Yahoo sites. They start at $0.47 and bottom out at $0.05:

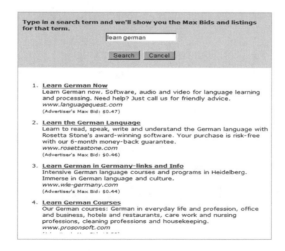

Of course, this is Overture, not Google. At the time of this writing, positions on Yahoo's search pages are determined by bids and bids only, whereas on Google you get preferential treatment for having an especially good clickthrough rate. And the competition, and the nature of the traffic, are different.

Not a problem. The Bids Tool is a quick gauge of how good a job advertisers are able to do on making money from their Yahoo clicks. In this case, nobody is willing to pay more than $0.47 per click. That tells you something already. When you compare "learn German," which maxes out at $.47, to "home mortgage," where Overture bids top off at over $4, you've got a sense now of how lucrative the learn-German market is, or is not, going to be for you.

SEARCH SMARTER WITH GOOGLE'S KEYWORD TOOL

Google has a keyword research tool of its own. To find it, click on the "Tools" link in the green strip at the top of your screen. Now you have two choices: If you've already got a full web site up and you don't want to start completely from scratch in guessing at all the keywords that are there, click on the "Site-Related Keywords" tab and simply enter the web address for one or several pages on your site. Google will search the site and come up with your keyword list for you.

However, if you want to reach people with keywords that you know aren't obviously found on your web site, click the "Keyword Variations" tab and enter one of your core keywords. Google doesn't just give you variations of that keyword. Check the tiny box to the right marked "Use synonyms," and it also gives you a host of related suggested themes. This is no hack job, either. Google's results here are just the results you'd expect from a world-class search engine.

Some of the results you'll find immediately relevant; others you won't have use for:

But Google gives you plenty more still. They won't give you the explicit numbers of searches for these terms on their system, but they will show you the relative amount of traffic they generate. To see this, click on the "Show columns" dropdown menu and select "Keyword popularity":

The partially-shaded rectangles tell you how saturated with competitors each keyword is, along with the relative volume of searches each term gets.

Yet another clever feature is "Global search volume trends," a month-by-month graphic of the average searches your term gets. We ran this feature for the term "Christmas," and it shows the dramatic increase in searches for November and December, and suggests a load of related keywords:

Very clever. And very helpful. You get variations that Overture couldn't give you and information about your competition that you can't get from any other free service. And it doesn't cost you a penny extra.

FIND EVEN MORE PAYING "MARKETS" ON WORDTRACKER

Now if you use Overture's tool to find all of the searched-on variations of "learn German," then every result it lists for you will have those two words in it:

1,371	learn to speak german
916	learn german free
598	learn german online free
383	learn to speak german for free
108	learn to speak german online
100	german language learn online
73	learn swiss german
71	learn german software
69	learn german cd

But aren't there people who want to learn German who don't use that exact phrase?

Sure are. There's also "study German" and even "study in Germany," not to mention the occasional guy who on a lark types in "learn Deutsch" or even "sprechen sie Deutsch."

But how do you know what other possible keywords there are? Answer: Wordtracker's Wide Search.

Let's say now that you're bidding on keywords for cell phones. Go to Wordtracker, and you'll get these suggested variations:

mobile phone
nokia
cellphone
cellular phone
ringtones
wireless
sony ericsson

> samsung
> sanyo
> motorola
> bluetooth
> accessories

MAKE MORE MONEY TAKING A DIFFERENT ROUTE WITH YOUR KEYWORDS

Let your imagination wander a bit, and you'll realize that these keywords that Wordtracker gave you could take you into new markets you never would have considered. More than a few people have figured out after looking over keywords and traffic that they'd make more money selling *accessories* for Nokia phones than being a reseller of the phones themselves. There are countless examples of this kind of surprise discovery. That's why you do this research in the first place. Keep an open mind!

Wordtracker is not designed to give you click costs or profitability estimates. It's made to alert you to all of the possible directions you can take with your keywords. It does this by

- showing you all the variations people have typed in over the last 60 days, and
- telling you the number of searches each one has had through Dogpile and Metacrawler.

That's what you get when you do a deep search. Here are the results for "cellphone":

Searching...300 row(s) returned
Taken from all Dogpile & Metacrawler queries over the last 90 days.
Click here to add all keywords to your basket

Keyword (?)	Count (?)	Predict (?)	Dig (?)
cellphones	1219	1575	✎
cellphone	649	839	✎
unlocked cellphones	350	452	✎
cellphone rental	229	296	✎
cellphone accessories	213	275	✎
cellphone wallpaper	209	270	✎
cellphone wallpapers	201	260	✎
prepaid cellphones	179	231	✎
free cellphones	155	200	✎
cellphone reviews	144	186	✎

You'll notice, of course, that other than including plurals along with singulars, this list doesn't give you any other spelling variations, like "cell" or "cell phone" or "cellular." You'll have to do those separately.

USE KEYWORDS TO OUTSMART YOUR COMPETITORS

Now if in fact every keyword is a market of its own, that means that four things are true:

1. Each keyword gets its own unique number of searches.
2. Each keyword converts differently to sales.
3. Each keyword has its own level of competition.
4. Each keyword represents something slightly different that folks are thinking when they type it in.

Stephen Juth has put together a tool called AdWord Acceleration (www.AdwordsAcceleration.com) that helps you pick apart your competition. Pick any keyword and run a search on it with this tool. You'll instantly see how the clicks, the cost, and the competitors are all different:

More about the significance of those quotes and brackets in a minute. But it's already clear just from this set of keywords which ones are going to be more valuable to you.

But notice that the exact-match version—the one in brackets—has four times as many advertisers competing for space, that it's lower on the page, gives you *one-fourth* as many clicks per day as the phrase match, but costs you 12 percent more on average to be there. *Your competitors don't know this!* Without tools like this in your toolbox, you'd likely miss this fact completely.

SOMETHING ELSE YOUR COMPETITORS DON'T KNOW

Now for a marketing insight from a different language: Mandarin Chinese. I sell a book in Taiwan and mainland China that teaches you how to learn Mandarin Chinese through your environment. It's a whole-life *Zen* approach that my customers insist is actually a tremendous resource for folks learning any language anywhere. Here are some of the search terms people use to find it:

> learn chinese
> speak chinese
> mandarin
> learn mandarin
> mandarin chinese
> learn mandarin chinese

Just the thought process alone behind each of these search terms is different. The person who types in "learn Mandarin Chinese" is already being more clear and specific than the person who types in "learn Chinese."

How so? The former is someone who knows that he does *not* want to learn Cantonese, the dialect spoken in Guangdong Province and Hong Kong. You've already got a more self-aware thinker on your hands, and someone with a different set of questions and challenges in mind than the person who's thinking more generically about "picking up a little Chinese." Never mind the different mindset for the person who types in "study Chinese" instead of "learn Chinese." Think about it.

Your market is the same way. Every keyword represents a different mindset, a different set of needs, a different personality. So how do you know who is who? You can poll the visitors searching on the different keywords. At www.AskData base.org, you can set up surveys and questionnaires in which you ask people specific questions about what they want or need, and then trace their varying answers back through the different keywords they found you on. More on this in a second.

NOBODY TYPES IN JUST ONE KEYWORD

This is a strategy taught by our associate Glenn Livingston, who has a comprehensive method for researching a market before you actually dive into it (www. Glenn-Livingston.com). Glenn points out a key fact about different keywords and how they represent different kinds of thinking: People don't usually just type in one keyword, find what they're looking for immediately, and quit. They type in a series of keywords. So, for example, a person might type in "learn Chinese" at first, and then go back and type in "learn Mandarin" to get more information and see more options. Or it might be the other way around.

So if you can capture the full attention of a person typing in the *first* in a series of searches, you've intercepted him and saved yourself from being pitted against other competitors on his next search.

KEEP YOUR GUINEA PIG FROM SMELLING

Glenn explains this principle well. He's become known around the internet as "the Guinea Pig Guy" for his web site www.GuineaPigSecrets.com. After doing careful surveys and ask campaigns, he discovered that the number-one question bugging the folks who typed in that particular keyword was, "How do I keep my guinea pig and his cage from smelling?"

Knowing that, Glenn incorporated a lead-in to that very issue in the headline of his landing page just for people who came to his web site via that keyword and increased his sales significantly.

You'll win with Google's editors when you hit on that *explicit conversation.* You'll win with your customers, as Glenn did, when you hit on that *implicit conversation.*

This is true of online marketing because it was first true of *offline* marketing. It's a principle of human nature that dates back to the days of bows and arrows, flint and fire. Whether you're selling goods and services by using a web page or by direct mail, or if you're simply trying to persuade another person to see your point of view, you speak directly to what he or she is thinking, both explicitly and implicitly.

When a guy tells you he wants to lose 50 pounds, he's probably not lying to you. But there's something even he doesn't realize: He really wants to lose 50 pounds *and* still be able to stop at Krispy Kreme every morning, get Burger King every day for lunch, and sit on the couch watching TV every night with a beer and a bag of Ruffles.

Sorry if this sounds cynical, but it's the advertisers that speak to *both* wishes who sell the diet pills and weight loss shakes and appetite suppressants, over and over again, year in and year out.

So you're aiming to hit people on *two levels.* There's the "explicit conversation" in their minds, which is the exact keyword they typed in. It's what you want in your ad and, if at all possible, on your landing page. Google will even reward you for doing this with your ad by offering you a lower minimum bid and giving you better positioning on the page by convincing Google's computers that your ad copy is more relevant.

Then there's the second level, the "implicit conversation" in their minds, which is unique to each keyword, the secrets of which you may not discover until you've talked to your customers and done the research. Glenn did that with his guinea pig site, and he's now impervious to competition.

It's when you hit that second level that your clicks turn into more sales. It's at that second level that you become impervious to ignorant competitors who don't understand your customer the way you do.

MORE MARKETS, MORE CASH: GET BEYOND THE OBVIOUS KEYWORDS

You know about Overture and Wordtracker, and we've already talked about AdWord Accelerator as a great tool for sorting out the real competition among keywords and bid prices and singling out the best-performing ads. There are others that give you a different emphasis and have features of their own that make them unique and very much worth having. AdWord Analyzer is one (www.AdWordAnalyzer.com). Keywords Analyzer is another (www.KeywordsAnalyzer.com).

In your toolbox out in the garage you need a Philips and a flathead screwdriver, not just one or the other. The same is true of these major keyword tools. Each one has its use, and owning more is like having a bigger toolbox.

And there's more to learn still. The first list of keywords you come up with, even if it's a long one, will be incomplete. AltaVista once reported that 20 percent of all its searches were totally unique in the history of AltaVista. You never know what people are going to hunt for. So here are some fresh ideas:

1. You'll want lots of *synonyms* and related subjects in your stockpile of keywords so that you can be sure you're reaching people who are looking for what you've got.

2. You can try bidding on *brand names*, though you'll have to work through the copyright issues yourself. Google has had a score of its own legal headaches as a result of allowing AdWords users to bid on trademarked names. Nevertheless, names of companies, magazines, associations, famous people, and famous places may all relate to your product. For example, for "billiards" you might bid on the name of famous pool player Jeremy Jones. For drums you might bid on "Buddy Rich."

3. *Misspellings* are a big opportunity, because so many advertisers don't bid on them, and the clickthrough rate is often higher. For my Lord of the Rings promotion, "Tolkein" (misspelled) got twice the CTR of "Tolkien" (spelled correctly).

4. LexFN.com is a web site that I find extremely useful and interesting. It's an elaborate thesaurus that uses web technology to find a scores of synonyms and related concepts.

    For example, here are LexFN's results when searching on the term "billiards." You'll note the long list they give you. This can be a very fun site to play with!

billiards	➡	pool
billiards	➡	nitride
billiards	⬅	break
billiards	⬅	cannon
billiards	⬅	carom
billiards	⬅	masse
billiards	⬅	masse shot
billiards	⬅	miscue
billiards	⬅	table game
billiards	⬌	billiard
billiards	➡	rudolf walter jr. wanderone
billiards	➡	william frederick hoppe
billiards	➡	william mosconi
billiards	➡	joe davis

If you just bid on the obvious generic version of a keyword like WalMart and you don't bother with other variations like Wal-Mart and Wal Mart,

Google's "expanded phrase matching" feature will attempt to match this for you, and usually succeed. However, those clicks will almost always cost you more money than bidding on the exact keyword. It's better to bid on the exact variations, the same way people type them in. Here are some examples:

Keyword Variations

Variations on Nouns:	*Variations in Hyphenation:*	*Adjectives:*
Shoe	Email	Mini
Shoes	e-mail	Large
	e mail	Red
Variations on Verbs:	firetruck	Blue
Drive	fire truck	Green
Drove	fire-truck	Cheap
Driven		Premium
Driving	*Variations on Names:*	Budget
Steer	Tolkien	2006
Steering	Tolkein	Used
Steered	J.R.R. Tolkien	New
	JRR Tolkien	
Wrong Apostrophes:	John Ronald Reuel Tolkien	
Driver's	John Ronald Tolkien	
Tire's	John Reuel Tolkien	
	John Tolkien	

---

5. *Glossaries and indexes.* We recently built an AdWords campaign for a client in which we went out and got a book on his subject. We went through the glossary and the index and used a large number of these terms in the glossary as keywords. Most of these cost only $0.05 a click, and they get a serious amount of traffic.

Multiply Your Keyword List by Knowing the Local Geography

Sometimes places are associated with businesses. For example, if you had a casino you might get additional cheaper traffic bidding on "Niagara Falls" than merely bidding on "Casino."

For *local* businesses, take whatever keywords apply to your business and then add your state and as many close-by cities as possible. For example, a Cincinnati IT firm might use this list, which includes suburb names and deliberate misspellings of "Cincinnati":

> Ohio computer consultant
> Cincinnati computer consultant
> Cincinati computer consultant
> Cincinatti computer consultant
> Tri-state computer consultant
> Tri state computer consultant
> Eaton computer consultant
> Jamestown computer consultant
> Miamisburg computer consultant
> Sidney computer consultant
> Troy computer consultant
> Milford computer consultant
> Loveland computer consultant

Go to a map site and paste in a list of cities, then use an Excel spreadsheet to mix and match those terms. Use "computer consultant," "IT company," "IT consultant," etc.

Once again, having *lots* of keywords is the key to untapped markets, low bid prices, and higher clickthrough rates. Your effort in this will pay dividends.

Use Quotes and Brackets to Uncover Cheaper, Less Competitive Keyword Niches

There's a way you can multiply your keyword list threefold and at the same time bid on terms that your competitors are overlooking.

Quotes and brackets hide more surprises than you'd realize. Stephen Juth's tool AdWord Acceleration (www.AdWordAcceleration.com) helps you identify which of these variations will cost you less money and where there's less competition to fight through.

Now as you're slogging through the sometimes tedious job of trying to come up with an exhaustive list of keywords, you may overlook a singular here or a plural there or forget a synonym or two that are closely related to one of your niche phrases. Google has already foreseen this problem and provides an extra feature, Expanded Phrase Matching, which adds singulars and plurals, similar phrases, and relevant synonyms to your keyword list for you. You'll need to be careful here, however. This service will work for broad-matched keywords in your list, but it won't work for phrase matches or exact matches.

Broad-Matched Keywords

When you insert keywords at the time you're setting up your campaigns, these are the keywords that don't have any delimiters around them. For example:

> used cars
> japanese used cars
> used cars for sale

You need to be cautious, because if you don't provide negative keywords, that keyword phrase "used cars" will show your ad for all of the following searches:

> used cars
> german used cars
> used cars cleveland
> used police cars

It may even show your ad for this wonky search:

> cars used in filming dukes of hazzard

Phrase Matches

These keywords are placed with quotes around them. For example:

> "used cars"
> "japanese used cars"
> "used cars for sale"

These will make your ad show in searches that include these terms in this order, without extra words inserted, such as the following:

        used cars

        old japanese used cars

        used cars for sale chicago

Your ad won't show for this search, however:

        used police cars

Exact Matches

These keywords are placed with square brackets around them. For example:

        [used cars]

        [japanese used cars]

        [used cars for sale]

With these keywords, only people who typed in these exact phrases, in this order, will see your ad. None of the following keyword searches will show your ad:

        used cars chicago

        german used cars

        old japanese used cars

        used cars for sale chicago

        used police cars

THE MATH OF NEGATIVE KEYWORDS: ONLY GOOD NEWS FOR YOUR CTR

Remember that if you include negative keywords in your lists, you'll pull down the number of impressions that your ads get because they'll show for fewer searches, which means that your CTR will automatically go up. But notice the math of this: If you could pull down your number of impressions by 20 percent, your CTR would improve not by 20 percent, but by 25 percent. Likewise:

- If you cut unwanted impressions by 30 percent, your CTR will increase by 42 percent.
- If you cut unwanted impressions by 40 percent, your CTR will improve by 67 percent.

- If you cut unwanted impressions by 50 percent, your CTR will double.

Negative keywords won't affect the CTR of exact-matched keywords, but they will help your CTR on phrase- and broad-matched terms. If you manage them the right way, there's no way they *can't* help.

Imagine getting the same number of clicks as before, but because your CTR is double what it previously was, Google gives you your clicks at half price!

GET A STEADY STREAM OF TRAFFIC FROM ULTRA-GENERIC KEYWORDS EVERYONE IS IGNORING

There was a time when you could get top position on high-volume, nonspecific keywords like "China" or "business" or "running" or "headache" for as little as $0.05 a click. If you did a Google search on one of these terms, only one or two results would show up, telling you that clicks were available for ultra cheap.

But advertisers had a very hard time getting a generic term like "running" to stick, especially in the early days before phrase- and exact-match options were available. A person who typed in a keyword like "business" could have any of a thousand completely different ideas in mind for what he was looking for, so he was not only unlikely to click on your ad, but even if he did click on it, he was that much less likely to buy anything from you.

Now the rules have changed. There's no longer a minimum CTR, so maintaining a certain number of clicks isn't an issue. And advertisers are much smarter now than they were even two years ago and are turning these generic terms into profitable information marketing opportunities.

So there's now value in bidding on generic, nonspecific, high-traffic keywords. But how do you make them work?

- Run trials, test copy ideas, and try again, writing ads until one works. This can take a long time, and you may fail a number of times before you find a winning formula. But you'll *win by attrition*, if you can keep testing and testing until something works.
- Make full use of negative keywords.
- Include statements in your ad that disqualify people you don't want. If you offer "Free Golf Instruction" in your ad, you may get riff-raff that you may not want. If you offer a "$49 Golf Video" you'll get people who will seriously consider purchasing it, and few others.

- Market information, not just products. Send people to a landing page that collects opt-ins, and offer a free guide, a tutorial, or an e-mail course of some kind, which will establish you as an information source, create longer-term customers, and grow your visitor value to where even the most generic clicks are worth getting.

THE KILLER SECRETS

You've learned some invaluable principles here:

- Literally every keyword in your list is a market of its own.
- Every keyword represents a mindset that people have when they type it.
- Behind everything explicit that your customers type in when they're searching, there's some want, need, question, or assumption, that they have (but may be completely unaware of).
- Some keyword markets are bigger than others.
- Some keyword markets are more competitive than others.
- Some keyword markets produce more dividends for the winners than others.
- There are always keywords that are overloaded with competition, where bid prices are jacked up far beyond their real market value.
- At the same time, there are always other keywords that are overlooked but which represent better, more responsive markets and which you can find if you use the right tools.
- You sell when you match that implicit conversation that your customers have with themselves.

A roundup of keyword research tools, with reviews of their pros and cons, is available at www.perrymarshall.com/supplement.

HEADLINES AND KILLER COPY FROM *COSMOPOLITAN* MAGAZINE: GET PAID TO LEARN FROM ANYBODY

I can't say I actually *like* Cosmopolitan magazine; after all, under the guise of supposedly liberating the modern woman, they've degraded her, turning her into a manipulative, greed-driven, appearance-obsessed, fashion diet sex slave.

But every now and then when I'm at the grocery store, I still buy a copy. Why on earth? Because these are the best headlines and writing formulas in the publishing business. The fastest route to writing a good headline is to simply steal one from *Cosmo*.

Last month I met with a client and spent most of the day developing a direct mail piece. They sell boring industrial hardware. It would put most folks to sleep, literally. But I brought copies of *Cosmo* and *Redbook* with me to assist. And it was an amazing process. The guys in the room thought we were crazy—until we started to actually apply the formulas. They were amazed at how well it works.

Here's what *Cosmo* did for us:

Cosmo Headline	**Our Headline**
The New Panties He'll Flip For	**The New Fuel Additive That Top Mechanics Flip For**
Brittany Murphy She's So Different Than You Think	**Linux** It's So Different than MCSE's Think
Be a Sex Kitten This Summer Hair, Makeup & Body Tricks to Make You Look Hot as Hell	**Be a Speed Demon This Summer** Project, Budget & Staffing Tricks to Make Your Operations Scream
"A Little to the Left" How to Say What You Want in Bed Without Bruising His Ego	**"Budget Cuts Again?"** How to Challenge the CEO Without Losing Your Job
Did the Man of Her Dreams Murder Her? Cosmo Investigates	**Did Bad Polymers Cause The Firestone Fiasco?** ACME Company Investigates

All of these speak directly to issues that engineers—or *Cosmo* readers—think about on a daily basis, sometimes an hourly basis. We just echoed those issues right back at them. It's a method that works for you time and time again. Oh, and if you'd like to use this approach without forking over $5 for a *Cosmo* every month, just visit www.Magazines.com and click on the magazine covers to get a full-size view.

Uncle Claude Sez

The purpose of a headline is to pick out people you can interest. You wish to talk to someone in a crowd. So the first thing you say is, "Hey there, Bill Jones" to get the right person's attention.

So it is in an advertisement. What you have will interest certain people only, and for certain reasons. You care only for those people. Then create a headline which will hail those people only.

We pick out what we wish to read by headlines, and we don't want those headlines misleading. The writing of headlines is one of the greatest journalistic arts. They either conceal or reveal an interest.

CHAPTER 6

Write Google Ads that Attract Eyeballs, Clicks, and Earn You Money

Your Google ads are an army of 100,000 tiny salesmen traversing the entire planet for you. And you only have to pay their salaries when the customers crack their doors open to listen to them.

■ ■ ■

Advertising is *selling in print*. That means the words you should use in your Google ads are the same words you use when you're on the phone or sitting across the table from a prospect, convincing him to buy something.

Before you try to write advertising copy, you should try to explain what you're selling to someone who might buy. And then, when they raise their eyebrows and lean forward, pay attention to what you just said.

My friend and mentor John Carlton, one of the highest paid advertising copywriters in the world, spends weeks researching his clients' product or service, going from person to person or business to business, gauging their reactions and questions. John learns what buyers really want and the certain turns of phrase that make or break the sale.

My own web site sports a perfect example of this. I offer a CD called "Guerilla Marketing for Hi-Tech Sales People" (www.perrymarshall.com/gm), and the title of this CD came about exactly this way. I was walking a trade show floor wearing a speaker badge a couple of years ago and people would ask me what I was speaking on.

I tried a few different titles: "21 Secrets of High-Impact, Low-Cost Marketing," "The Cold Call Curse," "Advertising Strategies for Technical Sales." But the one that provoked positive reactions was "Guerilla Marketing for Hi-Tech Sales People." And that's what it has been ever since.

Those tiny Google ads will succeed for exactly the same reasons. The only challenge is your limited space. Remember, the headline is 25 characters or less, and each line of the body is 35 characters. The web site URL displayed in the ad can also be up to 35 characters long.

So those are your limits. And that's okay, because your goal is not complex: just be *clear, simple,* and *relevant.* Claude Hopkins understood this well:

> *Literary qualifications have no more to do with it than oratory has with salesmanship. One must be able to express himself briefly, clearly and convincingly, just as a salesman must. But fine writing is a distinct disadvantage. So is unique literary style. They take attention from the subject . . . . Fine talkers are rarely good salesmen....Successful salesmen are rarely good speechmakers . . . . They are plain and sincere men who know their customers . . . . So it is in ad writing.*

English majors and Ph.Ds, and even MBA's generally suffer from severe marketing debilitations. In advertising, an academic education is more of a liability than an asset! You don't need to be a literary genius. Google Ads are the language of the street, not the ivory tower. Speak to your customer in the language she responds to in everyday conversation, and she'll click.

RIVETING TO YOUR CUSTOMER, DEAD BORING TO ANYONE ELSE

Just like in print advertising and on web pages, your headline swings the biggest difference in response. It's in that split second reading of your headline copy that your customer first makes up his mind whether you're really relevant.

Start with that keyword your customer just typed in and fit it into your headline. That will be the first signal to him that you're truly relevant. This means that you'll want to create enough different ad groups that each of your major keywords can have an ad of its own.

Let's say that you sell customized power supplies. There's certainly more than one way a potential customer of yours might come looking for what you sell. She might search for "adaptors." She might search for "power supplies." She might search for "transformers."

So you'll go to your major keyword tool, such as Wordtracker or your special keyword generating software, and you'll come up with all of the possible major variations and related terms for your market niche. Then you'll separate them out into smaller groups that you can match to specific ads. For example:

Custom Power Adaptors

Record-Speed Custom Production Time
Get a Full Quote in 1 Business Day
XYZAdaptors.com

> adaptor
> adaptors
> ac adaptor
> power adaptor
> custom adaptors

Custom Transformers, Fast

Inventory Cost, Lead Time Advantage
Get a Quote in One Day or Less

> transformer
> transformers
> power transformers

electrical transformers

voltage transformers

Power Supplies to Order

Inventory Cost, Lead Time Advantage

Get a Quote in One Day or Less

XYZAdaptors.com

power supply

power supplies

switching power supply

dc power supplies

ac power supply

These ads aren't very flashy, are they? They're not loaded with over-the-top language; in fact, to folks like you and me they're, frankly, boring. But that's okay. They aren't meant for the average guy on the street.

This particular company caters to engineers. These ads speak the language that engineers would understand, relate to, and appreciate. They match their audience just fine. And they get a good clickthrough rate. (Too good, in fact.)

Using your major keywords in your headline and creating as many different ad groups as you need with all of your biggest keywords is what makes the formula work.

WHEN YOUR INNER SALESMAN COMES ALIVE

After your headline, you've still got a second chance to convince your customer even further that you've got what he wants, and get more clicks. This is where your inner salesman comes alive.

There's a second secret that makes this work. Check out the difference between these two ads:

Popular Ethernet Terms

3 Page Guide—Free PDF Download

Complex Words—Simple Definitions

www.bb-elec.com

0.1% CTR

Popular Ethernet Terms

Complex Words—Simple Definitions

3 Page Guide—Free PDF Download

www.bb-elec.com

3.6% CTR

The second ad got *36 times* the number of clicks as the first! What happened? What was the secret? Look closely at the two ads. They both have the exact same wording. There's only one difference between them. What is it?

The first ad listed features and offers first, benefits second. The second ad listed benefits first. This secret is just as true in long-copy print advertising as in those little thumbnail Google ads. Features and offers are what your product has or what you're going to do. They describe it, what it includes, and how big or small or robust or thorough it is. Benefits, on the other hand, are the emotional payoffs your customer gets from using your product. So the list of *features* for an e-book you sell may include these items:

- 12 timeless principles
- 24 chapters, 222 pages of rock-solid content
- 64 full-color photos
- Helpful, easy-to-read charts and graphs
- Step-by-step tips and instructions
- Fascinating stories, anecdotes, and personal experiences
- Introduction by Bill Gates
- Etc.

But your list of *benefits* will tell your customer how she'll actually be helped by what you've written. Sometimes there's a little bit of crossover between these and the features:

- Achieve a 46 percent improvement in less than 30 minutes.
- Reach your goals in one-fourth the time using the 80/20 principle described in Chapter 5.
- You can apply any one of these 12 techniques immediately, and see instant results.
- Catapult Energy Levels, Convert Fat into Muscle, Develop Strength, Endurance, and Flexibility all at the same time.
- Discover how making *more* mistakes along the way becomes a strategy in itself that will grow your skill level even faster.
- Get compliments from your friends as they ask you again and again (jealously), "What has *happened* to you?"

There's no way to pack all of this kind of content into a Google ad, granted. But the principle of dividing benefits from features is universal. Your Google ad is about benefits (emotional payoffs) more than anything else. And when you describe benefits *and* features both, it virtually always serves you to put benefits *first.*

The second ad did exactly that. Switching the order gave us a 3,600 percent improvement! We know this because we tested it. Will it work this way in your market? That's for you to find out.

You don't have to be a poet or a master copywriter to convince your customer that he or she will get something of value. State your case simply and clearly, and test to see if putting the benefits up front and the features second will boost your response.

CHOOSE THE RIGHT URL TO DOUBLE YOUR AD'S EFFECTIVENESS

Imagine what different kind of message is sent by these two otherwise-identical ads:

Tough Marriage Struggles?
Get the Answers You Need to Start
On the Road to a New Life Together
HealYourMarriage.com

Tough Marriage Struggles?
Get the Answers You Need to Start
On the Road to a New Life Together
www.unmc.edu/academic/marital

That second ad suggests to me a kind of disconnect here, and that I'm in store for an academic discourse from some ivory-tower professor. Not what I'm looking for. The first one, on the other hand, tells me that this is exactly the kind of site I need to visit if I'm having problems with my marriage. It suggests a real human being who understands my issues on a personal level, not just an academic level.

People are surprised all the time to discover how much positive difference it makes to have a display URL that retells your story. Again, this is part of convincing your customer that you are *relevant.*

This display URL is the second most visible element in your ad. If you don't already have a winning web site address, then go to whatever source you can find (e.g., www.GoDaddy.com) in order to get new domain names that you can test against the one you're currently using, and see how much of a difference in CTR they actually make.

Remember, Google doesn't require you to display in your ad the exact URL of the page that you're sending traffic to. Your display URL can be different from your *destination* URL, as long as both of them resolve to the same place.

It's enough to tell people your domain name and nothing more, as in the HealYourMarriage.com example above. Use whatever actual destination URL you need to get them to the exact page, but the address you display can be shortened, to make it easier on the eye.

Test other variations like these in your display URL:

- www.HealYourMarriage.com
- HealYourMarriage.com
- www.healyourmarriage.com
- www.HealYourMarriage.com/Forgiving

THE "GOLDILOCKS THEORY": WHY THE BEST ADWORDS ADS ARE NEVER OVER-THE-TOP

We thought we'd get ultra-creative one day, and we wrote up an in-your-face ad that would shock Google users into clicking. We were just sure it would work. After all, the number-one worst thing you can do is bore people, right?

Here's what happened. It's the second ad below:

D.I.Y. Sales Leads

Don't hire telemarketers
Make prospects chase you instead
www.perrymarshall.com
42 Clicks | 1.0% CTR

Escape Voicemail Jail

Get Customers to Chase You Instead
with Savvy Guerilla Marketing
www.perrymarshall.com
20 Clicks | 0.3% CTR

We thought it was great. Our customers didn't. This happened again and again, and we learned a valuable lesson:

Google users do not generally respond to hype. Nor do they respond to messages that are too plain. What works is something in the middle—intriguing, yet not pushy.

Andrew Goodman, the author of *Winning Results with Google AdWords*, calls it the "Goldilocks" principle. Not too hot, not too cold—you want the temperature to be *just right*.

A DIFFERENT KIND OF "OVER-THE-TOP"

Here's an ad that was very bold, *and* performed well at first:

Prospecting Sucks
Make B2B clients call you first
with smart guerilla marketing
www.perrymarshall.com
1.1% CTR

Disapproved

Until Google's editor saw it and *disapproved* it. They don't let you use inflammatory words like "Sucks" or "Hate." They did let us get away with the word "stinks," however:

Prospecting Stinks
Telemarketing Annoys People
Guerrilla Marketing is King
www.PerryMarshall.com
1.3% CTR

SOME ALL-TIME MOST SUCCESSFUL GOOGLE ADS

These will surprise you. The ads that bring in record-high numbers of clicks are never the most flashy, the most outlandish, the most brilliantly composed copy you'll find. Never. They're simply a function of saying the right thing at the right time to the right people.

Here are some real-life examples of ads that our coaching clients wrote—ads that brought in record-high clickthroughs. You'll notice how unspectacular their language is, how they're specific rather than general, how they never completely follow all of the "rules," and how they're sometimes not even the best English!

But these have been tested *rigorously*. We worked and worked with our coaching students to help them create a message that perfectly matched what their customers were looking for, and their high CTRs show it:

Light Folding Tables

So Strong and Durable you get an
Unconditional Money-Back Guarantee
www.mobiliteuk.com

24.5% CTR

David Morgan
Oxford, UK

Kona Condos for Sale

Big Island MLS and Agents
Search Property Listings
www.MarylRealty.com

18.2% CTR

Claudia Hafner
Waikoloa, HI

The Lupus Recovery Diet

New Book! Learn how I overcame
Lupus without drugs or supplements.
www.LupusRecoveryDiet.com

9.5% CTR

Jill Harrington
Mill Valley, CA

Mens Hair Growth Solution

25 Facts You Don't Know About Your
Hair Growth Problem. But Should!
HowToStopHairLoss.com

25.1% CTR

Ed Keay-Smith
South Perth, WA, Australia

WHAT TO DO WHEN A HIGH CTR IS *NOT* YOUR GOAL

Your Google ads are an army of hardworking salespeople whose job it is to bring as many of the best prospects as possible to your web site. But you don't want just anybody. You don't want tire kickers; you don't want the looky-loos. You want genuinely interested people. After all, you have to pay every time they click.

Sometimes you find yourself in a very crowded marketplace attempting to single out the small percentage of people you know are a real fit for what you offer. That was the case with the adaptors example we showed you earlier. The business we were promoting provides custom-built electrical adaptors, converters, and transformers for high-tech Original Equipment Manufacturers, and only deals in large-quantity orders.

You can imagine how many different types of people go looking on the internet for adaptors, converters, or transformers in any given day. Even after we've used negative keywords (as we talked about in Chapter 4) to filter out the searches that we don't want, such as Transformer toy robots or online dollar-to-yen currency converters, we've still got people searching for the same terms we're bidding on who aren't looking for what we offer.

The guy who's just looking for a replacement power adaptor for his personal IBM laptop, for example. He's not our man. So it's up to our Google ad to filter out the rest of that traffic, to get as many *good* clicks as possible but as few of every other kind. More is not merrier.

The key is being clear and specific. We're going to write an ad that addresses precisely the type of customer we're after:

AC/DC Converters for OEMs
Qty 250+, Rapid Custom Production
1-Day Quote & Overnight Delivery
XYZAdaptors.com

This ad won't win any awards for high CTR or stunning copy, but it knocks out three criteria: (1) it's for people wanting *custom* design, not off-the-shelf, (2) it's for original equipment manufacturers (OEMs) only, and (3) it's for orders of 250 units or more. A lot of people are going to see this ad and pass it up. And that's okay. All we want are clicks from people who match these criteria. The ad will do its job.

Again, there's no black magic. Just tell your story. Be clear, straightforward, interesting, customer-centered, and most importantly, relevant. Sell on the computer screen just like you'd sell in person. People will see that you're for real, and they'll click and buy.

IF THE GUYS AT THE BAR WILL BUY IT, YOU'VE GOT A WINNING AD

Dan Kennedy tells the story of the highly paid, highly sought-after copywriter who writes sales letters aimed at blue-collar men. Before he delivers a project, he takes the draft down to the neighborhood bar, buys a round of drinks for all the guys, and reads them the letter. Then he gets their comments.

They chime in and tell him to tweak this, fix that, change the wording here or there. But he knows he doesn't have a winner yet until one specific thing happens:

> *One of the guys in the group asks where they can get what the letter is offering.*

That's when he knows he has a sales letter that's working. That's when it's ready for press. He's moved them from being critics to being buyers, and they don't even realize it.

Take your copy—your Google ads, your sales page, your direct mail pieces, your e-mail blasts—and test them in other environments, other venues, with friends, or out on the street. When people are salivating over what you offer, then you've got a winner.

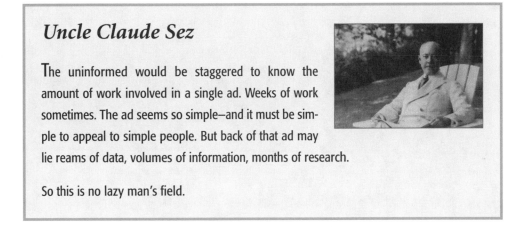

Uncle Claude Sez

The uninformed would be staggered to know the amount of work involved in a single ad. Weeks of work sometimes. The ad seems so simple—and it must be simple to appeal to simple people. But back of that ad may lie reams of data, volumes of information, months of research.

So this is no lazy man's field.

As Uncle Claude says, Google advertising isn't for lazy people. However, high performance ads can run with zero maintenance for months, even years. (Yes, even on the internet!) There are few assets more valuable than a system of effective ads that deposit money in your bank account 24/7/365.

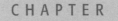

CHAPTER 7

Triple Your CTR—No Genius Required

T esting, testing, testing. The way to make your CTR move into triple digits is to try, try again. Subtle modifications to your ad can make the difference in the number of clicks you receive. This chapter will explore this phenomenon.

■ ■ ■

AdWords rocket scientist Howie Jacobson kicked off a new campaign a couple of years ago, driving sales people to his site where he teaches them how to turn cold calling around into a profitable sales process. He started out with a simple Google ad:

Stop cold calling forever

Small business marketing system.
Free report and 2 chapter download.
www.leadsintogold.com
33 Clicks | 0.8% CTR

Today he's making traffic scream with killer ad copy that has more than *tripled* his clickthrough rate:

Cold calling not working?

Discover a powerful alternative.
Free report and 2 chapter download.
www.LeadsIntoGold.com
368 Clicks | 2.7% CTR

What's Howie's secret? He's just brilliant, right? A copywriting genius, a Merlin, a sorcerer of the printed word, no? Howie will tell you no. (We think he's brilliant, as does every one of our customers who consults with him on their Google campaigns. But for this example he would argue otherwise.)

Seriously, what was his secret? Answer: Howie just tested ad copy. That's all he did. You've seen the first and the last of his ads, but you haven't seen the score of other tests that he ran, that inch by inch grew his CTR by tiny percentage points over a two-year period. Here are just a few samples of the ads he put up for testing:

Stop cold prospecting.

Small business marketing system.
Free report and 2 chapter download.
www.leadsintogold.com
42 Clicks | 1.0% CTR

End cold calling forever

Small business marketing system.
Free report and 2 chapter download.
www.leadsintogold.com
430 Clicks | 1.7% CTR

End cold calling forever

Attract customers automatically.
Free report and 2 chapter download.
www.LeadsIntoGold.com
145 Clicks | 2.0% CTR

End cold calling forever

Lead generation system explained.
Free report and 2 chapter download.
www.LeadsIntoGold.com
338 Clicks | 2.2% CTR

Howie's full collection is available at www.LeadsIntoGold.com/genius. When you look over these ads, you see nothing spectacular: no shocking content, no in-your-face power words that jump off the page, no mind-blowing sales hooks.

Even more importantly, if you looked over all these ads by themselves and tried to *guess* which one would get the most clicks, I'll bet you couldn't. Not among these ads. *Only the market could tell you which one would be the winner!*

Howie knows his customers quite well, but he never had any brilliant flashes of insight, and he never consulted on these ads with any of the geniuses of the copywriting world. Frankly, they couldn't have helped him anyway.

Instead, he did what all successful Google advertisers do: He ran two ads at a time. He compared their results. He deleted the loser and wrote another ad to try to beat the winner. He followed his nose, people clicked on what resonated with them, and the market told him what worked. As the saying goes, "It is a fool who looks for logic in the chambers of the human heart."

The magic of AdWords is that nobody sensible sits and ponders an ad before clicking on it. A person sees your message, his brain runs an instant gut-reaction 0.1-second process, and the decision is made. He clicks, or he doesn't.

It won't do you any good to pontificate long hours over ad copy. Calling in focus groups to sit and discuss their feelings and reactions is a waste of your time, and theirs. In the Google world, people's decisions are instantaneous, and you can never predict with 100 percent accuracy what the market is going to react to. Your good common sense will tell you what should work. And then the market will tell you what actually *does* work.

SET UP A SPLIT TEST

Google lets you do this with ease. When you've got an ad written, you can write a second one as well, just by clicking on the "Create new Text Ad" link next to the ad that you're currently running. Google will rotate this with your other ad, and you can compare the clickthroughs, eventually delete the loser, and try to beat your best again:

ELECTORAL VOTES VS. GOOGLE VOTES: IS YOUR WINNING AD REALLY A WINNER, OR DID IT JUST GET LUCKY?

Everybody remembers the 2000 election when George Bush and Al Gore spent weeks in limbo over the Florida recounts. Then it almost happened again in 2004. Ohio was right on the hairy edge. Two elections in a row, Americans went to bed not knowing who the new president was going to be.

On the morning of November 5, 2004, I sent the following e-mail to my subscribers:

> Friends and neighbors, here we are with yet another cliffhanger election. The presidency is tottering in its edge in the state of Ohio.
>
> Mr. Bush has 2,767,158 votes (51.4 percent) and Mr. Kerry is behind with 2,589,499 votes (48.1 percent).
>
> But Kerry still has a very slim chance at winning.
>
> And yes, that slim chance does matter. Terms like 'statistically significant' sound pretty mundane, until the most powerful office in the world is at stake!
>
> Well if you do Google AdWords the way I teach it, your best two ads are always competing in their own election too, just like Mr. Bush and Mr.

Kerry are today. You ***always*** create two ads instead of one and you always tally up the votes to see which ad is the winner and which one is the loser.

This is your #1 strategy for improving your CTRs and cutting your bid prices over time. Little changes make a BIG difference.

For example:

> **Simple Self Defense**
> For Ordinary People
> Easy Personal Protection Training
> (0.8%)

> **Simple Self Defense**
> For Ordinary People
> Fast Personal Protection Training
> (1.3%)

You just change 'Easy' to 'Fast' and the votes go up almost 50%!

So . . . was the winner really the winner? Or was it just luck?

That's what John Kerry needs to find out. And if it's important to him, it's important to you in your Google Ad Election, too. That's why I created a no-cost web utility, just so you can test your ads and find out if the winner was really a winner, or just lucky.

It's at www.SplitTester.com—you enter the CTR of both of your ads and the number of clicks. It tells you whether it was pure dumb luck, or if you're 80 percent sure, 90 percent sure, 95 percent sure, or 99 percent sure the winner is really the winner.

I entered the Bush-Kerry results in www.SplitTester.com—Bush, 2,767,158 clicks and 51.4 percent CTR vs. Kerry, 2,767,158 clicks and 48.1 percent CTR and it says 'You are approximately 99 percent confident.'

99% IS good enough for your Google Ad, but it's not good enough for Mr. Kerry today—he's looking for 100 percent. But whether you're testing your Google ads, your landing pages, or whatever, savvy marketers always make sure they're sure. Because the election on Google may be just as important to YOU as El Presidente is to the Nation.

To Your Success,

Perry Marshall

Statistical Significance: Sounds Boring, but It's Really Important

During our personal AdWords coaching program last summer, I got a very frustrated e-mail from a member whose sales had gone south, not north, since the program started. Not exactly what he was hoping for when he signed up, right? (Especially since we make outrageous performance guarantees to students who are accepted.)

This gentleman was getting a few sales a day and was re-writing his sales page also on a daily basis. He'd get two sales on Tuesday and assume the changes were bad, he'd change something, then he'd get five sales on Wednesday and assume the changes were good.

But little by little his sales started going down the toilet, heading toward zero. By the time he sounded an alarm he was in dire financial straits. Furthermore, he hadn't saved the early versions of the sales page when it *was* working, so it wasn't even possible to go back to what was working.

About a month later he let go of his employee and shut the business down. As they say in Spanish, ¡Qué lástima!

Again, by the time we found out about this, it was too far gone to save. Here's what he failed to do:

1. He didn't use our SplitTester.com tool to figure out if his winning sales page was really a winner.
2. He didn't keep a detailed record of his modifications and copies of all the versions along the way.

This problem applies to *anything* you test—not just Google ads, but opt-in pages, sales pages, etc.

When you do split test, how do you know when you've got enough results to be sure that your winning ad didn't just "get lucky" or the loser didn't just have a bad day or a bad week? How many trials do you need to run?

THE SPLIT-TESTER TOOL AND HOW TO USE IT

With the help of our friend Brian Teasley (www.Teasley.net), we created a split-testing tool on the web, at www.SplitTester.com. With this tool, you can find out how likely it is that it was luck. Here's how this works.

Let's say we've got two ads. One gets a 1.2 percent clickthrough rate with two clicks total, and the other gets a 2 percent clickthrough rate with five clicks total. Was the better one really better, or was it luck? Let's see:

Enter Your Numbers Here:			
Number of Clicks (First Ad)	1.2	Number of Clicks (Second Ad)	2
CTR (First Ad, in %) *	2.0	CTR (Second Ad, in %) *	5
* Your CTR must be entered as a simple percentage. For example, enter 3.1% as "3.1", and not "0.031"; Enter 0.7% as "0.7"			
	Calculate	Reset	

When we click "Calculate" it says:

> You are *not very confident* that the ads will have different long-term response rates.

But now let's say we've got 20 clicks for 1 and 35 for the other, not just 2 and 5:

Enter Your Numbers Here:			
Number of Clicks (First Ad)	1.2	Number of Clicks (Second Ad)	20
CTR (First Ad, in %) *	2.0	CTR (Second Ad, in %) *	35
* Your CTR must be entered as a simple percentage. For example, enter 3.1% as "3.1", and not "0.031"; Enter 0.7% as "0.7"			
	Calculate	Reset	

We click "Calculate" and it tell us:

> You are *approximately 95% confident* that the ads will have different long-term response rates.

Ninety-five percent confidence means that if we ran this test 100 times and got these results, the results would lead us in the right direction 95 times. That's pretty good. I'm willing to bet on those kinds of odds.

Here's a real simple rule of thumb: When your response percentages are fairly close between two competing ads, you need 30 or more responses to each one before you can declare a winner. And maybe even 50. But if one is already doing considerably better than the other, then it doesn't take as long—after 10 to 15 actions have been taken you can be fairly sure. Use www.splittester.com to find out.

When you do proper split testing, when you test two things side by side and make sure you're 90 percent, 95 percent, or 99 percent sure of your results before you go on, you're dealing with hard numbers and good, high levels of certainty. Your progress isn't squishy and uncertain; it's measurable and reliable.

Not only does that make for very effective marketing, it makes for a healthy company, good morale among the troops, and a happy bank account.

Uncle Claude Sez

Now we let the thousands decide what the millions will do. We make a small venture, and watch cost and result. When we learn what a thousand customers cost, we know almost exactly what a million will cost. When we learn what they buy, we know what a million will buy.

We establish averages on a small scale, and those averages always hold. We know our cost, we know our sale, we know our profit and loss. We know how soon our cost comes back. Before we spread out, we prove our undertaking absolutely safe. So there are today no advertising disasters piloted by men who know.

CHAPTER 8

Triple Your Traffic with Site-Targeted AdSense and Google Image Ads

There's even more traffic waiting for you on Google's content network, through image ads and on targeted sites. Test it to find out if you can make it profitable. You could potentially double or triple the number of quality visitors to your site through these new venues of advertising.

■ ■ ■

I've always been leery of AdSense traffic. When I start a new campaign I almost always turn it off. You should too, because it throws off your split tests. You get an uneven mix of Google and syndicated traffic in your ads, and you can't compare the CTRs. Furthermore, it usually brings lower quality visitors who are less inclined to buy.

Usually. But not always! Sometimes AdSense ("content targeted") brings *better* traffic.

A couple of years ago I had a project that was running on Google traffic alone. I'd tested and tweaked the ads, and I thought it was doing OK. Then one day, almost by accident, I turned AdSense on. It produced a sudden *avalanche* of traffic. Good traffic, too. The number of visitors to that web site grew by a factor of five times!

Many of our customers have been able to double, triple, even quadruple their traffic just by turning on content-targeted sites in addition to the regular Google and search network traffic. We just always recommend that you get your traffic working and profitable on Google all by itself (no search partners, no content targeting) before you jump onto the content network.

IS SYNDICATED TRAFFIC PROFITABLE?

First, set up Google's conversion tracking feature on your site, which we explain in Chapter 16, and then run your traffic for a few days, weeks, or even months until you get a solid number of clicks and conversions. Then you can tell if your cost-per-conversion has you in the red or in the black:

Often customers will tell us that they turned on AdSense traffic, which ran up a huge bill for them, but it didn't result in a single extra conversion or sale. That may be your experience, too, so be ready.

I had a different experience on one of my projects. I experimented to see if the profitability of AdSense traffic coming to my own site was the same for every ad group. Turns out it wasn't. It wasn't even the same for each keyword.

I found one single keyword for which AdSense traffic was profitable. Just one!

But this wasn't just profitable. *This one keyword on AdSense was accounting for 40 percent of my clicks and 60 percent of my sales.*

So don't give up! If your AdSense traffic seems a waste of money, dig deeper and find out if it's that way for all of your campaigns or only some of them. For all of your ad groups or only some. You may find just one keyword that brings you outstanding traffic from the content network, while all of your other search terms bring in nothing but garbage clicks.

TWEAK YOUR BID PRICES ON ADSENSE

Maybe you're already bidding on AdSense traffic and getting excellent conversion rates, but you're paying far more money for those conversions than you are for regular Google search traffic. Not a problem. Just bid less per click for your AdSense traffic.

Go into "Edit campaign settings" from your campaign summary view, and notice that on the right side of the page you've got a "Content bids" option, where you can set separate prices for content clicks.

Save your changes, and now you can go in and edit your content-targeted bid prices separately:

Bid a lower price, and now running AdSense traffic won't bankrupt you.

SITE-TARGETED ADSENSE CAN BE A MASSIVE GOLDMINE

You can choose what sites your ads show on. Some sites will bring you terrific traffic. Other sites, worthless. Look at the astonishing signup rate I got on one site I chose:

See that signup number for www.Friendster.com over on the right? That's a nearly 50 percent conversion rate! That one site multiplied my traffic and conversions *five times*. How would you like your traffic to grow by that amount? What could you do with five times the amount of traffic and sales?

SET UP SITE-TARGETED ADSENSE

You can click through to set up site targeting from your main campaign page:

After choosing your language and locations, write your first text ad. Google will now give you the choice of listing URLs that you want to target. Also enter keywords to describe the topics you want to find relevant web sites for. Entering a longer list of keywords can only help your cause. You can even choose age and income groups you want to reach.

Next, choose your sites.

Here's where the metrics differ from regular keyword bidding. You set your bid price. You're fixing a cost per thousand impressions rather than per-click.

Now Google gives you a group summary that shows you that different set of metrics:

The bottom line on site-targeted AdSense:

1. You're still aiming for the highest CTR possible. The $0.25 cost-per-thousand (CPM) minimum means that at a 1 percent CTR, that's $0.025 per click. At a 0.1 percent CTR, it's $0.25 a click. At a 3 percent CTR it's only $0.008 per click.
2. You can split test ads without regular Google search traffic interfering with your statistics.
3. This tool was designed with "brand" advertisers in mind. Nevertheless, a direct response marketer like yourself can get tremendous use out of it, if you watch your numbers and conversions carefully.
4. Image ads usually get much higher CTRs than text ads, so take advantage of those whenever you can.
5. Just as with Google search traffic, the key to success is always constant, patient split testing of ads!

MAKE SITE-TARGETED ADSENSE WORK BETTER

Do you want your sites to click and convert better for you? The *peel and stick* method is the answer, again. It's just that this time you're not peeling and sticking keywords; you're peeling and sticking targeted web sites. This way your ads more closely match the content of the sites that you're advertising on.

You delete a web site from one ad group, insert it into a new ad group, and write an ad that matches the thinking of the folks who are coming from that site or group of sites. That's means you want to understand the people who are coming from those sites: their hang-ups, their psychology, their wants. Then again, that's exactly what you do with keywords, isn't it?

Because with site-targeted ads you're no longer mixing results and statistics from regular Google, search, and AdSense traffic, when you create ads and they start to show, the comparison with any other ads you've been showing is direct, apples-to-apples. You can compare the clickthrough rate of one ad with the click-through rate of another without having to factor in all of the vastly different types of places that it's being served.

Now what's going to determine your success at the end is your *cost per conversion*. How much does it cost you to get a real customer? That will tell you whether you're hitting or missing.

In the example I showed you earlier, the nearly 50 percent conversion rate I got meant that I was paying less than $0.25 for each conversion (visitors to opt-in e-mail addresses), whereas in my regular Google traffic ad groups I was paying more than $0.50. So I knew it worked.

Now you've got one more new way of slicing up the online world.

WHAT ADSENSE ADS AND TURN-THE-CORNER KEYWORDS HAVE IN COMMON

With regular Google search ads, you're trying to be there for the people who are looking for you. With AdSense the psychology is different: you're now writing ads to *interrupt* people.

This is also the case for turn-the-corner keywords, which we talk about in Chapter 21. Those are the keywords you bid on to position yourself as an alternative. You know, selling Austria tours to people who are looking for Swiss vacations. This psychology of interruption permeates AdSense advertising.

Banner ads have always worked that way. Knowing how to create effective image-based banner ads to run on Google's networks is yet another way to multiply your clicks.

IMAGE ADS

This is one of the few places on earth where you can create an image ad entirely on your own, have it run as the only advertisement on a web page, and (when it's AdSense you're running) pay only when people click. The first thing you need to know is that *size does matter*. You've got a choice of multiple sizes for your ads. And it's no surprise that the larger ad sizes will earn you more clicks. They're more invasive, more noticeable. Tiny strip-ads squeezed in at the very top or very bottom of the page are less so, and likely to bring you a lower CTR.

Good copy brings clicks, but don't assume that multiple ads of varying sizes are performing differently only because of their copy. Size can be the bigger determiner. Split-test pairs of ads in the same size categories. Run ads in all of the sizes that Google makes available. Otherwise, your numbers may only tell you which size is most likely to draw clicks.

Higher Clickthrough Rates

Surprise. Image ads earn better CTRs than regular content-targeted text ads. And not just the big ones, either. Even the smallest image ad can average a clickthrough rate two to three times that of a text ad. The biggest reason for this is that visuals are always more impulsively compelling than mere words. Plus with image ads there's less competition; you may be the only Google advertiser that's showing on a particular page.

The flip side to this is that your image ads will get fewer impressions than text ads. There's simply no way that image ads can be served as frequently as text ads. Here's what happened in one campaign that we ran over ten days:

Text ad:
240,625 Impressions
1,925 Clicks
0.8% CTR

120x600 Image ad:
6,000 Impressions
66 Clicks
1.1% CTR

728x90 Image ad:
23,667 Impressions
213 Clicks
0.9% CTR

468x60 Image ad:
6,429 Impressions
45 Clicks
0.7% CTR

300x250 Image ad:
1,594 Impressions
51 Clicks
3.2% CTR

You saw it right: the largest ad got shown the least. Web pages are like real estate, and space can be costly. The text ad got shown *40 times more often* than the other image ads!

It's not unheard of for some image ads to pull in CTRs *ten times as high* as text ads with identical copy. But even with their good CTRs, image ads get shown much less, and because of their impulse appeal, the traffic they bring in tends to be lower quality and won't convert as well to sales.

GOOGLE WON'T LET YOU EMBARRASS THEM

When you introduce a new image ad, it could take several weeks before Google begins to serve it. So sit back and be patient. Why the wait? Because Google's editors have to approve it first, and they're *doubly cautious* about what kinds of images they syndicate. With text ads, this sort of thing is less of an issue.

The last thing Google wants is the embarrassment or legal juggernaut of unwittingly farming out image ads with offensive or shocking content to other sites. Have all your image ads ready to submit up front. Have at least two ads with different copy and content in each size so that you can split-test their effectiveness. And be prepared for a long wait before Google's editors get around to okaying your ad.

MAKE MONEY HERE WITH THE SAME TIME-TESTED PRINCIPLES

So what about copy? Fundamentally, the same principles of good copywriting apply to image and banner advertising as to regular Google ads. In a lot of cases, you can copy a text ad over to a banner ad, tweak a couple of phrases to make them complete sentences, and you're done.

The point is to be relevant, compelling, and credible. You already know that from regular Google ads. Still, there's a good deal that you can test:

- Stating specific numbers and statistics
- Including a very brief testimonial with a name

- Using more in-your-face, compelling language
- Adding a small visual, even a graph, that supports what you say in your copy

Take these ideas and combine them with the wild variations in ad copy we share in Chapter 20, and see what makes the click rate on your image ads soar.

Uncle Claude Sez

Pictures in advertising are very expensive . . . . Anything expensive must be effective . . . .

Pictures should not be used merely because they are interesting, or to attract attention, or to decorate an ad. Ads are not written to interest, please, or amuse. You are writing on a serious subject—the subject of money spending . . . .

Use pictures only to attract those who may profit you. Use them only when they form a better selling argument than the same amount of space set in type.

CHAPTER 9

Local Ads on Google: Beating the Yellow Pages

A giant fraction of Google searches are local. Advertise your business locally and you'll get traffic and customers for a fraction of the cost of other media. This may sometimes reach more people than Yellow Pages ads; it's more traceable than billboards, and it costs you less than mailings and fliers.

■ ■ ■

According to the Kelsey group, 60 percent of all internet searches are local. Some estimates run as high as 75 percent. But even if it were only 20 percent, that's still a *lot* of searches. Tens of millions a day, at least.

Whatever the number is, local search is undoubtedly the most untapped opportunity in Pay Per Click (PPC) marketing. You want to sell weight loss plans, MP3 downloads, high definition TVs, or mortgages nationwide on Google? You can do it, but you'd better strap on your gladiator helmet and prepare for a fight. But if you're an accountant, plumber, painter, repair shop, or podiatrist, it's an easy victory. In most local markets, your internet competitors have no idea what they're doing. Rarely do they read a book like this.

For example, my friend Bill is a minister who does weddings, and he gets more business than he can handle, bidding $.50 on simple terms like "wedding officiant." His wedding officiant brethren aren't exactly the green berets of the marketing world.

This is also a great place to consult, setting up campaigns for neighboring businesses, because it's so underserved. Think about it:

- Hundreds of local businesses in your city spend upwards of $1,000 a month just on Yellow Pages ads, so these people are already spending money!
- The Yellow Pages reps are also selling Internet Yellow Page listings, creating more awareness of online marketing. But they're not selling Google ads on Yahoo.
- Companies like Google are so busy dealing with existing opportunities, putting reps on the street to sell PPC to local businesses is a *long* way off at best. (There are rumors of partnerships with Yellow Pages companies though.)
- In categories where mail order is impossible and you *have* to get it locally, the clicks are *cheap*. For example, right here in Chicago, there are only six ads showing for the keyword "Brake Shop" and one of them is eBay. Nickel clicks, anyone?
- Web savvy local advertisers are *very* rare, and this is not going to change any time soon. Running a retail store and running an online store are two entirely different things. So for local yokels, it's like I always say, "In the land of the blind, the man with one eye gets to be king."

If you can accept the fact that many keywords will only produce a few local clicks a month, the return on investment (ROI) on what you do get is extraordinary.

GOOGLE ADWORDS VS. OTHER LOCAL ONLINE SERVICES

My friend Glory the dentist got a call from the local phone company a few weeks back, offering her the chance to advertise her practice online. Shoppers in town, the rep told her, would jump on the internet looking for dentists in the area, and her name and contact information would show up when folks clicked through to look at the directory.

Here was the deal: the phone company charges $0.25 for every click, and then posts a special private phone number that web visitors can use to call her office. Her cost per call: $15.

Glory wanted to know what I thought. I said a smart marketer like her, using Google, can get new customers far cheaper than paying $.25 per click *plus* $15 for every phone call she gets.

When I opened up my computer and showed Glory how Google advertising works locally, we did a search on "dentists," and sure enough, there appeared the local phone company's Google ad (!) right up top:

Dentists & Dental Offices

Find a dentist here in town in
your online XYZ Yellow Pages
www.XYZYellowPages.com

In other words, it's buying clicks from Google wholesale, sending them to its directory, and selling those second clicks to dentists retail. Not to mention the extra $15 Glory would have to pay per phone call. Sound like a good deal to you? Didn't think so.

Now any advertising is a good deal if it brings you new customers at an acceptable ROI. You shouldn't reject an "acceptable" ROI from ad media B even if you get "extraordinary" ROI from ad media A. Still, Glory can bring local customers to her dental practice without having to go through the phone company's system.

She can buy clicks for the same price as the phone company, probably less, and take people directly to her own site rather than a directory where she's one of a dozen other listings. She can put up a sensibly-designed, direct-response web site that turns visitors into phone calls and appointments, *without* having to pay $15 for every call!

The fact that a service is charging some dentists $15 a call should tell you something. Heck, maybe you should start a service like this and only charge $10.

Google uses IP addresses and other clever technologies to figure out where people are when they search, and it serves up local ads. (Its targeting seems to be pretty accurate too.)

Local Google is perfect if you're in any of these markets:

Real estate	Beauty salons	Heating/Plumbing/
Hotels	Telephone service	Electricity
Private investigators	Attorneys	Landscaping
Wedding planners	Bid auctions	Doctors
Storage	Cars & trucks	Counselors
Home furnishing	Printing	Restaurants
Dentists	Construction	Clothing
Churches	Movers	Photographers
Hospitals	Funeral planning	

YOU'RE REACHING TWO KINDS OF PEOPLE, NOT JUST ONE

It seems like we give the following advice to real estate people the most, but the idea applies in a lot of places. There are *two* kinds of people looking for your business:

1. A person who lives in your area—your city, your state—who types in "real estate," "dentist," "churches," or "restaurant" and expects that the results he sees will be area-only. You'll be there when he comes looking for you.
2. A person may not be in your area at all (or else Google's system can't tell where he is), but is still asking for your area's services. He goes to Google and types in "movers in Palo Alto," "Palo Alto real estate," or "hotels Palo Alto," hoping to get Palo-Alto-only results. He may be traveling on holiday; he may be planning a move; he may be an investor.

He may in fact be from Palo Alto. But he could be down in San Diego. Or way out in Orlando. Or in Montreal. Or Sydney, or Tokyo. But he's still searching on Google for you, and he identifies Palo Alto by name.

Either way, you want to be there, ready to open the door when he comes knocking.

REACH THE FIRST PERSON

Because you're aiming at these two kinds of people, you can set up *two* Google campaigns for them, not just one. So here's how. When you're first setting up your campaign, select regional targeting like this:

Then you choose your country, followed by your state/province, and even a city or group of cities. This particular ad campaign is targeted at the United States, and specifically at two metropolitan areas in New York State:

From this point forward, everything else you do in this campaign is the same as is described in the rest of the book, but your ads will only be seen in the local area you choose.

REACH THE SECOND PERSON

If you were advertising for real estate in California, you'd set up a *nationwide* campaign, possibly even an international campaign, but with local terms like "Visalia real estate" and "Yorba Linda real estate." After all, there are likely to be people from all over the country, and maybe even outside the country, who are doing searches on these terms.

So you'd grab a map or a listing of cities from a web site and create a keyword set like this:

> California real estate
> LA real estate
> Healdsburg real estate
> Villa Real real estate
> Santa Monica real estate
> Buy homes California

> Buy homes San Francisco
> Buy homes Bakersfield
> Buy homes Sausalito

To do this the best way, you would combine a large list of general keywords (the same ones you used on the regionally targeted campaign) with a large list of cities and towns, and then use a spreadsheet to mix and match them together.

Either way, you'll end up with a huge keyword list: 95 percent of them will never get searches, and the other 5 percent may only get a few. However, it doesn't cost anything to bid on these keywords if nobody clicks, and when people do click, they'll only be five or ten cents. Not much traffic, but what you do get will be bargain priced. You should still buy generic keywords in your local campaign, but these local keywords in a nationwide campaign will bring very cheap clicks, mostly.

Your real estate Google account would be arranged like this:

> Campaign #1: California Targeting Only
>   Group 1: Real estate
>   Group 2: Buy homes

> Campaign #2: National Targeting—entire USA
>   Group 1: California real estate
>   Group 2: Buy homes California

Now you have both bases covered, and you'll be getting as much traffic as possible for your local market. The key is that you're not leaving out people in other geographic locations who are seriously looking for what you offer.

You can also use your business's address or latitude and longitude, and target all searches within a radius that you select. Google even gives you the advanced option of choosing your own customized set of coordinates that you want to target.

HONE YOUR CHOPS ON A LOCAL TEST CAMPAIGN BEFORE YOU GO NATIONAL

An age-old advertising practice is to test ideas in a smaller market before you spend big bucks to try them out in a larger one. Nowadays, the risks of going national instantly if you have a good product may seem small because after all, you're paying for one click at a time, you can set a daily budget, and you can turn your traffic on and off at will. But that doesn't undo the value of trying your product in one small geographic area first.

For example, if you sell advice to investors, you might start just with investors in New York State. The advantage? You don't need to worry nearly as much about your daily budget. If your cash reserves are limited, you can choose this smaller market to start off in, and if in the first few weeks or months it's not profitable, you're not forced to shut the entire thing down for fear of quickly going bankrupt. Make the sales process profitable in a smaller market, and then go national.

At that point, you're able to take on the big boys in the worldwide market because you know that the mechanism works like clockwork in the small market, and every dollar you send out comes back with more dollars attached. Oh, this is also an excellent way to keep competitors from knowing what you're up to, if they don't live in the cities you're targeting.

OFFER A SERVICE LOCALLY BUT A PRODUCT NATIONALLY

Entrepreneur Frank Pasquale is a designer of handmade custom electric guitars. These are not the el cheapo variety you buy off the shelf at Wal-Mart. These are quality, handcrafted instruments that can sell for several thousand dollars apiece.

Frank lives in the remote suburban-Chicago village of Hampshire, and his custom clients are always local, because for him any one project involves personal visits, selecting woods, looking over neck types and paint samples, and giving ongoing feedback about the product as he assembles and fine tunes it.

But Frank uses Google to find his customers. He reaches musicians in Chicagoland who are doing general online searches for custom guitars, along with anyone around the country who may on occasion search specifically for guitar builders in the Chicago area.

Frank is in the process now of taking his local skill and spreading his knowledge literally around the world. That's the next step for him as his custom-work business gets off the ground. He'll be writing an e-book about custom guitar design, and he can sell it any place on planet earth where people are searching and interested.

And this is not just an information business, either. You can run your business locally, and at the same time make money teaching people worldwide how to do exactly what you do. And again and again you'll discover that they turn right back around and pay you to do it for them. After all, you're the professional. Your book proves it.

In Frank's case, people will buy his kit, and then turn around and hire him to design their guitar for them. That means this is going to generate customers and orders for Frank Pasquale's handiwork from around the country, and possibly even around the world, not just Chicago, as he instills in readers the confidence that *he knows custom guitars*. Sometimes it's easier just to pay the expert to do the job than to try and do it yourself.

The next thing Frank may do is use his credibility from his book to hire and train apprentices to design custom electric guitars themselves. Frank can then send them out to do their own work, and he can set up and manage their local Google campaigns for them for a fee, which then, like his own ad campaigns, will run on autopilot.

You can take this business model and replicate it many times over!

Uncle Claude Sezs

We usually start with local advertising, even when magazine advertising is better adapted to that product. We get our distribution town by town, then change to national advertising. Sometimes we name the dealers who are stocked. As others stock, we add their names.

Sometimes we name the dealers who are stocked. As others stock, we add their names. When a local campaign is proposed, naming certain dealers, the average dealer wants to be included. It is often possible to get most of them by offering to name them in the first few ads. Whether you advertise few or many dealers, the others will stock in very short order if the advertising is successful. Then the trade is referred to all dealers.

CHAPTER 10

Slashing Your Bid Prices: Google Rewards You for Relevance

People are drawn to you when you're relevant. The formula for success on Google is relevance. When you're relevant, people will click on your ads, Google will explicitly reward you for it, your costs will drop, and your profits will grow.

■ ■ ■

"Which one do you think will get us to the martinis faster?"

My friend and mentor Dan Kennedy was in a conversation over cocktails with an ad agency exec. The discussion was about two different ads that were each scheduled to run in a national magazine. One was the classic, Claude Hopkins formula with a compelling headline and dense, carefully-worded body text, followed by a call to action and a clip-out coupon to be mailed in.

The other was the ultra-modern, ultra-sleek gigantic full-page ad with the irrelevant photograph and blurb at the bottom in tiny, whittled-down, vague text about how hip XYZ Company was. The usual ad agency fluff.

Dan pointed to the old-school ad and explained to the ad exec that it had been run before, was carefully tested and tweaked for maximum response, and was virtually guaranteed to make the client's phone ring. "How would you like to run this one against your corporate-style ad and see which one got more sales?" he asked. "What would your client think?"

The ad guy chuckled. "To be perfectly honest with you, Dan, I could run either one. Makes no difference to me. But if I have the choice of showing one or the other to the CEO, which one do you think is going to get us to the martinis faster?"

Glitz and puffery are the secret sauce in most ad agencies. The goal is not ROI or to make the client's phone ring. The goal most certainly is not to be relevant. The object in an old-school ad agency is to goose the CEO's ego, get invited out for drinks, and get the guy to invite you back and write you another round of checks next month.

IT AIN'T HIS NECK UNDER THE GUILLOTINE BLADE

When you're the person laying out the cash yourself and it's *your own* business, *your own* risk, and *your own* credit card that Google is dinging every month, you don't have time for your own ego stroking. Your customers don't have the patience for it either. Nowhere is this more clear than in Google AdWords. Putting your own money on the line has a funny way of wising us up to what gets clicks and what doesn't.

GOOGLE REWARDS YOU FOR RELEVANCE

Traditionally, you get higher positions on the search page by bidding more. But when your clickthrough rate goes up, Google actually gives you better positioning without charging you more per click. It rewards you for being relevant.

Roughly speaking, the first position has always been given to the highest bidder. But Google has long maintained an ingenious little twist. Here's a simplified version of its formula:

Your Relative Position = Your Bid Price x Your Clickthrough Rate

The fuller version of Google's formula is your bid price multiplied by your Quality Score. (More on the Quality Score later.) Either way, your CTR swings the biggest difference apart from the price you bid.

Which CTR, exactly? *The CTR of your individual keywords as they perform on Google alone,* not the total CTR of your ad groups, not the CTR of any of your ads, and not the CTR of your ads as they're performing on Google's search partner sites or AdSense.

If you have a high clickthrough rate, then you don't have to bid as much for the position. For example, I bid $1 and my ad gets a CTR of 1 percent. Your ad gets a CTR of 2 percent. You can get the same average position as me by bidding $0.50. If you bid $0.51 then you'll get the position above me. If you're already in top position, Google will automatically charge you a lower bid price as your CTR improves. Not bad.

This really works. Our customers who buy our regular online book (www.Perry Marshall.com/adwords) tell us this all the time:

> Before I purchased your program, I was averaging about 50 clicks a day, paying at least 25 cents each for them. But after implementing your strategies: 402 Clicks, average cost per click of 14 cents, average position of 3.3 with my ads. My traffic is much more targeted, so my conversion rate almost doubled. I don't think my first impression of Santa Claus was this good!
> —Michael Mettie, Simple Streams, The Colony, TX

> My name is Andres Cordova, and I've been doing Internet Marketing for a little over four months now and I just have to say that your Definitive Guide To AdWords has been the best course I've bought because it has allowed me to spend a fraction of what I used to pay and get more than five times the visitors for less money. And I particularly love your newsletter, it's always filled with quality content.
> —Andres Cordova, Salinas CA

This isn't magic, even though it looks like magic. Our customers are just writing straightforward, relevant ads, and their cost-per-click is going down. That's what will happen to you. It means you're coughing up less money to Google every month, and you're putting more in your own pocket every day.

KEYWORD STATUS AND BEING RELEVANT?

In summer of 2005, Google advertisers panicked as Google started implementing a new policy of *keyword status*. Every keyword in Google's system now has a minimum required bid. It can vary wildly, from two cents up to a dollar or more in some markets.

If you won't pay that minimum for a particular keyword, Google will simply put your keyword on *inactive status* and won't show your ad when folks search on that term. Agree to bid the required amount or higher, and your ads will show.

Many watched as their precious five-cent minimum bids got jacked up to ten and twenty cents and more. Some who based their entire selling strategy on this minimum price thought it would kill their business.

It didn't. If Google deactivates keywords and demands higher bids for them, you've got two options, not just one: (1) Bid what Google asks, or (2) tweak the copy of your Google ad to convince Google's computers that the ad is relevant, thereby lowering the minimum required bid. Before you choose the first option, you had better be sure that it's necessary, and that you can afford it. If you're going to choose the second option—and we strongly recommend that you do—then the trick that works best is this:

> *Take the keyword and stick it into the headline of your ad.*

If you can't do that without screwing up the ad and making it a mismatch for all the other keywords, then do peel and stick. Take that keyword out of your list and put it into a new ad group by itself with an ad that uses it in the headline. That will convince Google's computers that you're writing relevant ads, and you are likely to be allowed to bid a lower price. More importantly, *you're all but guaranteed a higher CTR by doing this.*

It's an unfortunate fact that you're not really being judged on relevance here, you're being judged on *perceived* relevance. Google's system won't necessarily offer you a lower minimum bid price because you've got a high CTR; the system will only do so if it sees that you're using your keyword in the ad.

So when all is said and done, the test is not in whether you're *actually* relevant to consumers; the test is only in what Google's computers *think* looks relevant. Still, by setting up its system this way Google is now forcing you to do with your keywords and ad groups what successful advertisers already do: break everything down into small, tight groups.

Here's an example of how this looks when done right:

If you have keywords in your list that don't show up in the ad, Google may well penalize you by putting your keywords into *inactive* status.

WHAT WE SAVED BY DOING PEEL AND STICK

We did some testing, and here are some fascinating numbers we were able to dig up concerning Google's minimum required bid:

- If Google sets a minimum bid at $0.10, there's a 10 to 20 percent chance you'll be able to reduce that to $0.05 just by putting your keyword in the headline of your ad.

- If Google's minimum is $0.20, there's a 50 percent chance that you can put the keyword into the headline of your ad and get the bid down to $0.10.
- If Google requires $0.30 or more, peel-and-stick as described above will knock at least 30 percent off the required minimum bid.
- If Google requires $1 or more, peel-and-stick will typically knock 50 to 60 percent off the minimum required bid.

THE QUALITY SCORE SECRET FORMULA

How are Google's computers going to decide how much your minimum bid price is in the first place? It's through a formula that it calls *quality score*. Here's what it tells you about it:

> *Quality Score is determined by your keyword's clickthrough rate, relevance of your ad text, historical keyword performance, and other relevancy factors.*

Clever language on Google's part. Specific, and yet ambiguous.

It quotes four essential factors in its decision. Now the *clickthrough rate*, as far as we've been able to detect, actually makes little to no difference at all in Google's decision-making process.

By *relevance of your ad text* it means the question of whether its computers find your keywords in the text of your ad or not, which we call "keyword-to-adtext match." The *historical keyword performance* refers to how that particular keyword has tended to perform in all Google campaigns everywhere over time, in other words, whether it tends usually to get good clickthrough rates or bad, whether it gets a high number of searches, whether it's bid on by a large number of people, and how long on average folks have been able to make it "stick."

The *other relevancy factors* are the rest of the secret formula that Google just plain isn't going to share with you. These factors are probably too involved to describe in any concise way, since they relate to Google's tracking of user behavior and perhaps dozens of criteria.

But if we are to rank these four factors in terms of which ones make the biggest difference, it breaks down like this:

1. Historical keyword performance across Google
2. Keyword-to-ad text match
3. Other relevancy factors

4. Your CTR

So since you can't change how a keyword has always performed throughout Google's history, since your CTR makes little difference, if any, and since it's not going to tell you what those "other relevancy factors" are, you're left to tweak the text of your ad to include your keyword. But that pretty much by itself will earn you the ability to pay a lower minimum bid for a keyword.

CHARGING IDIOTS MORE MONEY TO BE IDIOTS

It used to be that Google would slow your keywords down, put them "on hold," and even disable them if your ads were lousy and your clickthrough rate was in the basement. But not anymore. Google now has Wall Street to please, and with enough advertisers begging to pay more, to do anything possible to let their keywords run again, the decision makers in Mountain View finally got wise and said yes. This now means that you're free to run perfectly irrelevant, utterly ineffective, poorly-constructed ads and ad groups through Google. It will just charge you more to do it.

How to See the Minimum Bids for All Your Keywords

To find out the lowest bid prices that Google will accept for each of the keywords in your ad group, click on "Edit Keywords" and then "Estimate Traffic." To set all of your keywords automatically to the minimum CPC:

- Use the "Find and Edit Max CPC" tool under the "Tools" section. One of the options is "Increase each keyword's Max CPC to the recommended minimum bid."
- Go to the Ad Group view, select all of your keywords, click the "Edit Keyword Settings" button, and then from the drop-down list that says "Prefill all keywords . . ." select the last option.

ACTING UPPITY WON'T EARN YOU A PENNY MORE

Do you like to see impressive, amazing things? Do you like to see jaw dropping, astonishing situations and events? Of course you do. Everybody does. And it only costs eight bucks. That's right, for eight bucks you can go to a movie theater and watch Jet Li, Denzel Washington, or Angelina Jolie deliver two solid hours of stunning imagery, special effects, action and thrills, splashed across the big screen in blazing color and Dolby Surround. And these days, with a few thousand dollars of audio-video equipment, you can see the same thing, maybe better, at home.

Yes, people like to be wowed and impressed, and Hollywood thinks nothing of spending $100 million on a picture so it can give the people exactly that. And it does a great job of it.

But one of the worst things you can do is deliberately try to impress your customers. Why? Because when you try to impress instead of building trust, educating, and persuading, your would-be customer shuts you off. Her guard goes up, and she stops listening to you. Help her solve problems and capitalize on new opportunities, however, and she's yours for life.

Most businesses these days are trying hard to impress. But impressing people never makes a positive contribution to customers' needs. Nobody cares how many billions of dollars of assets some company has. Your customers would much rather know that you'll go to the mat for them when there's a problem. They'd much rather know that you're there to help them.

Your customers want to be spoken and written to in a conversational, layman's tone of voice that strives to build trust with them, educate, and persuade them, rather than dazzle and impress. This is why the best of the best Google ads are seldom the ones that jump off the page and knock you over. The ones that get the most clicks are simple, engaging, straightforward, and honest, and they speak in a voice that their unique market recognizes and understands.

If you want CEOs to buy you martinis, New York ad agencies might be just your thing. If you want to stand tough against your competitors and sell to customers who trust you, just be relevant.

Uncle Claude Sez

Ads are not written to entertain. When they do, those entertainment seekers are little likely to be the people whom you want. That is one of the greatest advertising faults. Ad writers . . . forget they are salesmen and try to be performers. Instead of sales, they seek applause.

When you plan or prepare an advertisement, keep before you a typical buyer. Your subject, your headline has gained his or her attention. Then in everything be guided by what you would do if you met the buyer face-to-face.

Don't try to be amusing. Don't boast, for all people resent it. Don't try to show off. Do just what you think a good salesman should do . . .

CHAPTER 11

The Most-Ignored Secret Behind the Most Profitable Marketing Campaigns

I t's time to distill your message to its most salient point. Although you may think you have pared it down to a tight message, have you told your customers why they need to buy from you?

■ ■ ■

This could be the most important chapter in the whole book. Because this is the ingredient in marketing that trumps all others. With this ingredient, *everything* in marketing gets easy. Without it, people wander around in an aimless stupor for years.

What's this "thing," this magic ingredient? *It's having a good answer to the following question:*

> *Why should I do business with you, instead of any and every other option available to me, including the option of doing absolutely nothing at all?*

Another way of asking the same question is:

> *What do you uniquely guarantee?*

When you have a really powerful answer to these two questions, your ads practically write themselves. When you have a really powerful answer to these questions, people will line up to buy from you.

When your business possesses a simple, unmistakable mission, it stands out in an age of obfuscated marketing messages and Byzantine corporatespeak. Your answer to this question is your *unique selling proposition (USP)*. A statement of value that's so clear and focused it's almost impossible to *mis*-understand it.

Less is more. Your business will grow, the world will sit up and take notice, and even your Google ads will write themselves, when you stand out from the crowd with a clear, simple, and utterly unique message.

WHAT IS A USP?

Your USP is that one thing special about you that your customer can't find anyplace else. It's your *Unique Selling Proposition*. It's what you bring to the table that no other business does, or even can.

Your USP is about the uniqueness of your product, and it's more than that. It's your whole argument for not just your product but also its accompanying services, why it's necessary in the first place, and the timing of getting the product and seeing your problem solved now, rather than later.

A lot of the difficulties people have with Google come not from doing Google AdWords wrong per se, but from a USP that isn't clear or maybe isn't even unique in the first place. If you have your USP right up front, everything from the keywords and ads to the price of your product, all that falls into place.

IDENTIFY YOUR USP

Your first step is to answer these four questions:

1. *Why should I read or listen to you?*
2. *Why should I believe what you have to say?*
3. *Why should I do anything about what you're offering?*
4. *Why should I act now?*

In fact, these are a powerful guideline for what to include in your Google ad *and* on your web page when folks click through. Answer them, and you've taken your message and made it that much more compelling.

We've all fallen on our faces attempting to be all things to all people. *You can't please everybody.* If your purpose is murky and your sense of identity vague, it confuses your customers and robs you of time and energy.

Perhaps the most famous USP of all is from Domino's Pizza:

Fresh, hot pizza delivered to your door in 30 minutes or less, guaranteed.

This isn't unique now, but in the early days of Domino's, it most definitely was. A multibillion dollar business was built from this very unique, simple statement of value.

Just look at what a focused USP does in streamlining the daily routine for Domino's staff:

- *Fresh.* They don't have to keep freezers full of prepared inventory. They keep all of the needed ingredients on hand, along with adequate staff to prepare the orders. And the pizza doesn't even have to taste good.
- *Hot.* They keep a disciplined time schedule, getting the pizzas into the oven in time with orders that come in. They keep the right containers on hand and the delivery guys make sure the pizzas are well packed.
- *Pizza.* No spaghetti. No lasagna. No fine wines. No burgers.
- *Delivered.* This isn't an eat-in joint. No servers or extra busboys, no extra chairs or tables.
- *In thirty minutes or less.* Everyone works fast.
- *Guaranteed.* When the customer hears this, he sits up and pays attention. And the manager has financial incentive to keep the operation moving.

When you have this message defined and focused, it will *liberate* you. You become the specialist. People ask to you solve problems that you're not geared to deal with, and you simply refer them elsewhere. Nobody expects you to be an expert on anything other than your one niche.

You can certainly expand into other areas, and many businesses have multiple USPs. Every product in a retail store has its own USP. But in each case, it needs to be unique, and it needs to be clear.

A good USP will fit in a Google ad—or at least the most important part of it will. Here's an ad that turned up on a search for "pizza delivery":

1-800 PIES 2 GO
Great Pizza Delivered to your Door
Free call Fast Delivery Great Pizza
www.1-800Pies2Go.com

SAY IT IN JUST ONE SENTENCE: YOUR ELEVATOR SPEECH

You'll arrest the rabid interest of people in seconds with a good USP. When a guy asks you in the elevator what you do and you've got 14 seconds before you get off at the next floor, this is your answer. It's your *elevator speech*. Craft it right, and the guy will probably perk up and ask for your business card and web site.

Some great examples are:

I sell the world's best comprehensive health insurance plan to businesses with ten employees or less.

Health Insurance
Comprehensive Health Plans for
Businesses with 10 Employees or Less
www.SmallBizHealthInsurance.com/10

I help high-tech companies grow sales and eliminate waste with highly targeted web traffic, marketing, and publicity.

Generate Leads
Make Customers Call You First
Don't Sell Harder—Market Smarter
www.PerryMarshall.com

B2B Guerilla Marketing
Eliminate Cold Calls & Ad Waste
Instant Web Traffic & Free Publicity
www.PerryMarshall.com

I teach you how to find the love of your life in 90 days or less.

Find Love in 90 Days
Discover Your True Love & Life Partner.
Based On 30 Years of Research.
www.90DayMatch.com

Imagine how people will take notice of you when you have quick answers like these. We're all drawn to a simple, clearly defined, gutsy message. Hammer out your own, and you've got a verbal business card that's irresistible.

YOUR USP MAKES A GREAT GOOGLE AD

Last summer I went searching for a solution to my increasingly slow computer. I typed "my computer is slow" into Google, and this surprising ad popped up:

Slow Computer?
The Problem is Registry Errors.
Scan Your PC Now—Free Trial
www.RegistryFix.com

Registry errors are a common problem with Windows. Software that repairs these errors is available all over the place. But no advertisers that I've seen are as clear and gutsy as the guy who wrote this simple ad.

It got my attention. So I clicked. As did thousands of others. This advertiser sells software to fix registry errors. That's it. The diagnosis is uncomplicated, the offer is compelling—a free and quick, no-obligation registry scan—and the result is a faster computer. Can't beat that for clarity.

Can you take your message and whittle it down to one short sentence, enough to fit in a Google ad? Can you restate your USP to diagnose a problem and position yourself as the solution? It's amazing to us how many advertisers could, but don't. Be different. You'll get the clicks.

BUILD AN UNFORGETTABLE PERSONALITY AROUND YOUR USP

"Big Ass. Big-Ass Fans." It was of the funniest ads I've ever seen. The naked truth? It could easily be knocked off. But they get love letters. They get hate mail. And all the while Bill Buell and company have created a product with broad appeal and an incredibly unique identity in the marketplace. This is their amazing story.

HVLS Inc. of Lexington, Kentucky, builds large, slow moving fans for giant spaces like warehouses, dairies, and factories. The initials stand for *high volume, low speed*. But they're not known to most people as HVLS. Most people know them as Big Ass Fans. And they're taking their world by storm with some of the savviest guerilla marketing we've ever seen.

You read it right. They sell fans. Great big ones. Fans with blades literally wider than your house. Factory-sized fans, fans that take your breath away. But Big Ass Fans' marketing is not just "cute." HVLS's growth is literally in the *triple digits*. In a lousy economy where some industrial titans are having their worst stretch in decades, Big Ass Fans is rising like a rocket.

This isn't a terribly exciting product. It's not a magic portable DVD player. It's not some satellite receiver with built-in GPS. It's just a fan. But Bill Buell has created a personality around this product so powerful that it grabs people's attention immediately and *catapults* his advertising effectiveness into the stratosphere. Big Ass Fans is now a permanently recognizable brand.

More importantly, there's a real economic argument here. Let's say you've got a warehouse equipped with a standard fan, circulating air at 10,000 cubic feet per minute (cfm). Run it for one hour, and it would cost you 5.6 cents. But suppose that you needed to circulate 125,000 cfm of air, 13 times that amount. Using 13 standard fans would cost you $.75 an hour. Run those for 24 hours, and you've got a one-day electric bill of $18.

But run just one Big Ass Fan, and you'll circulate the same amount of air and do it for $0.88 a day. Sound like a good deal? Here's how it breaks down over time:

	1 Day	1 Week	1 Month	1 Year
13 Standard Fans	$18.00	$126.00	$540.00	$6570.00
1 Big Ass Fan	$0.88	$6.16	$29.12	$321.00

This is now part of Big Ass Fans' USP. It doesn't just shock you into buying the product. It *proves* that this is an investment. The question now becomes, can your warehouse afford *not* to put in a Big Ass Fan?

In Bill Buell's industry, vendors think it's a crime to stand out, to look different, conspicuous. Advertisers in industry magazines and trade journals work hard to keep their own ads looking just like everyone else's ads, which, of course, is marketing suicide.

We talked with Bill on the phone about this very question. "Most folks look at my ad," he explained, "and they think to themselves, 'Whoa, if I wrote ads like that, they would look totally different from everyone else's.'" Bill's reaction? "*Of course* your ads should look different from everyone else's. How else will they get noticed? That's the whole *point!*"

Want to dominate your market? Take your USP, add some serious chutzpah, and give it an unforgettable delivery.

A Good USP Literally May Save Your Life

In her landmark book *Nickel and Dimed: On (Not) Getting By in America* (Owl Books, 2002), daring journalist Barbara Ehrenreich tells of a risky personal experiment she undertook: abandoning her city, her identity, her education, and professional qualifications for three months, she attempted to live on $6 per hour working as a Wal-Mart employee, waitress, and maid in an unfamiliar city.

Ehrenreich discovered how it's barely possible to survive on those wages. She had to work two jobs. She constantly lived on the verge of homelessness, with no insurance and no safety net. And, not surprisingly, she was treated with little respect. She experienced the worst of everything.

While Ehrenreich showed great insight into the daily grind of America's "working poor," she offered little in the way of answers or solutions, other than a poignant appreciation of the hard-working waitress who pours your coffee at Denny's and the goodness of leaving a generous tip.

But see, here's the real problem: How is it that a person can go to school for 13 years, graduate with a diploma, and be qualified for nothing more than waiting tables or stocking shelves at Wal-Mart? Is $6 an hour all the value that a person gets from a modern high school education? Sadly, that seems to be the case. There is a missing ingredient.

If you have a USP to offer the world, you're not a commodity any more. The book *Nickel and Dimed* is not just about low wages, but about being a commodity. One hundred twenty-five pounds of "human capital." It's an awful state to live in.

One of Ehrenreich's jobs was working as a maid. In that industry if you want to be a bona fide cleaner of homes or businesses, you have to get bonded, and there are a number of hurdles you have to overcome. But what would prevent that same person from creating a clever USP, printing up a compelling flier, distributing it, and getting five or six families to employ her directly—for $20 per hour instead of $7—without having to go through the official hurdles? It's a free country, after all.

Aristotle Onassis once said, "The secret of business is to know something that nobody else knows." Don't let yourself become a commodity. Discover how to do something valuable that few others can do. That's not something you learn in a classroom of 30 kids. And the funny thing is, while you *will* learn that in a marketing seminar, unlike a traditional education nobody can give you your answer, your USP, on a platter. Your challenge is to identify it for yourself.

The lesson in all of this? The concept of a *unique selling proposition* is not merely a marketing technique, but in fact is a fundamental life skill, an essential ingredient in all human endeavors. It's as important as reading, writing, and 'rithmetic. And it's your ticket out of the rat race.

Uncle Claude Sez

A person who desires to make an impression must stand out in some way. Being eccentric, being abnormal is not a distinction to covet. But doing admirable things in a different way gives one a great advantage. So with salesmen, in person or in print . . . . There is refreshing uniqueness, which enhances, which we welcome and remember. Fortunate is the salesman who has it.

CHAPTER 12

How E-Mail Transforms Those Expensive Clicks into Profitable Customers

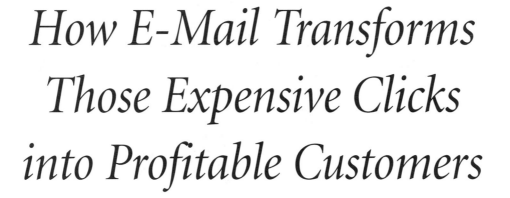

Use e-mail correctly, and your customers will stick around three times longer. It's the most personal online medium there is. With it you can sell to your customers again and again by building trust and creating an entire business around your own unique personality.

■ ■ ■

No discussion about Google AdWords would be complete if I didn't show you how to turn that expensive one-millisecond click into a long-term relationship. When someone clicks on your ad, Google charges you

$.50 regardless of what happens next. If the guy leaves after five seconds, he's gone, and you'll probably never get him back without paying *again*.

Fifty cents for five seconds of someone's attention—dang, that's $600 an hour! Kind of depressing if you look at it that way. On the other hand, if that person gives you her e-mail address, you can communicate with her on a regular basis for little or no cost. If you're trying to sell a $1,000 product, which is easier to get from your prospects: a $1,000 order or their e-mail address?

The more complex your sales process, the more important it is to break it up into bite-sized steps. Which is why the main Google AdWords page at www.perry marshall.com/google is an e-mail opt-in page:

Visitors can either opt-in or leave. I figure if a person's really interested in Google AdWords, i.e., likely to buy my *Definitive Guide to Google AdWords*, they'll at least give an e-mail address first. This is better than only getting e-mail addresses from people who buy the book on the first visit. And it's better than having only one shot at selling them our services.

PUT PERSONALITY AND PIZZAZZ INTO YOUR E-MAIL MARKETING

In a day when much of the manufacturing industry is downsizing, cutting management, laying off employees right and left, and moving in a panic to India and China, B&B Electronics in Ottawa, Illinois, is knocking over growth records right and left. It's hiring more staff to handle a growing number of incoming catalog orders and a mounting list of willing buyers.

Most people would never think to utter the phrase "infectious personality" and "electronics manufacturing company" in the same breath, but B&B is both. It refuses to surrender to the dull, corporate geek stereotype. Instead, it has loads of fun with it. B&B regularly courts its growing customer list's inboxes with witty, lively messages that celebrate the stale, geek image of the Dilbert-cubicle engineer. Marketing director Mike Fahrion graces customers with his regular "Mike's Politically Incorrect Newsletter" rant column.

A techie's girlfriend recently wrote Mike to thank him for turning the engineer stereotype on its head:

> Hey Mike,
>
> This is the hapless girlfriend who shares an e-mail account with a techie who subscribes to your newsletter.
>
> The amount of dry, poopey e-mails that we get in our inbox is criminal, and it's pathetic that the other electronic types are perpetrating the geek image that's out there by sending those incredibly boring messages.
>
> I mean, come on! "All you've ever wanted to learn about C++, Extensive Layer Management Plug-In for mental ray Pipeline"? BRUTAL!
>
> Thank you for the sense of humor in your newsletters.
>
> Mike—I think you need to start a 'how to write a cheese free newsletter course.' I can think of many companies that need your help!
>
> Signed,
>
> Disgruntled Dish

Does B&B owe its stellar growth in a stagnant industry all to its e-mail? No, but it's a vital ingredient of its carefully-thought-out marketing strategy. Mike understands this. (That's why he hired Perry to ghostwrite his Politically Incorrect Newsletter.)

Whether you're B&B Electronics or Martha Stewart, capturing a person's e-mail address turns a one-time click into an opportunity to build a relationship that can work for you again and again and again.

Buying Google traffic is only the first of many important steps in our marketing process. If we had to credit our own success to just one thing, it would be the use of e-mail and autoresponders.

THE POWER OF YOUR E-MAIL LIES IN BEING PERSONAL

Run-of-the-mill advertisers have little respect for the personal nature of e-mail. They don't realize how easy it is to turn off otherwise receptive prospects to their message, just by violating that.

You need to write to the person as one person. Unless the person you're writing to is part of a group where he or she personally knows each of the other members, then the last thing you want to do is write as though you're talking to a crowd. Talk to your customer, an individual.

1. A "From" Field that Shows You're a Real Person

If a personal approach works for the actual text of your e-mail messages, chances are that same principle will apply to other details in your e-mail. Such as your "from" field, for example. Consider the different impressions these "from" lines create:

> Bill Kastl
> William Kastl
> William D. Kastl
> Nakatomi Corporation
> William D. Kastl, Nakatomi Corporation
> Nakatomi Sales Department
> Bill Kastl, Nakatomi Sales

You want to be warm and personal without looking like spam. This is a challenge because spammers are themselves always trying to make their messages look like they're from some forgotten old friend. The key is to say something that is so specific to their particular interests they know no spammer would ever come up with it.

Pick a "from" field that your customers will understand, and stick with it.

2. A Provocative Subject Line

The most important thing about e-mail is that its success or failure is all about *context*. E-mail subject lines work *not because they follow standard copywriting formulas* but because *they tap into what specific people are interested in at a particular time.*

If I showed you generic examples of e-mail subject lines, it would be almost impossible for them to not sound like spam. So let's take examples from a specific context that *you* understand: Google AdWords. Here are the subject lines of some of the e-mails I've sent out to my Google AdWords customer list:

- When Google is NOT the Best Way to Get a Customer
- Are Google Employees Spying on You?
- Google's 'Don't Be Evil' and all that
- Five Insidious Lies About Selling On The Web
- Hurricane Katrina: I'll Match Your Donation

These headlines do not assault the reader with cheesy-sounding promos, but they do hint very strongly at a story. They provoke curiosity rather than scaring people off.

3. Everybody Loves a Good Story

B&B Electronics sells industrial communication hardware via catalog and the web. A "boring" geek business if there ever was one. But when Perry writes the monthly newsletter, he turns that dull, geek image on its head and interrupts a dreary day of engineering with wry humor.

His method? Storytelling.

> Subject: **ZIGBEE AND THE GEEKS' REVENGE**
>
> Leslye was the girl who made my heart go pitter-patter in junior high school.
>
> I was always sure to take the long way to Social Studies, down the stairs to first floor, past her locker, then back up to 2nd. Just checkin' up.
>
> I was not the boy who made her heart go pitter-patter. She liked Sam, and maybe Rodney too. She wasn't interested in me. And she never discovered that I liked her. It was my little secret.

Now maybe you didn't run the sound system in Junior High like I did. Maybe you ran the film projector instead. Maybe you programmed Apple II computers in BASIC and belonged to Chess Club.

Still, you and I were geeks, and the pretty girls took no notice of us.

But it's 2006 now, and we geeks rule the world. We're the people who really know what's going on. All the pretty boys and their material girls have viruses on their computers and they can't function without us. They're at our mercy.

And the latest Geek Revenge these days is...

ZigBee.

ZigBee is sort of like wireless instant messaging for sensors and smart devices. You drop ZigBee nodes wherever you want, no cables necessary, and the more nodes you have, the more communication paths there are and the more reliable your system is . . . .

This is a little wonky. It doesn't surrender to the stereotype that engineers are dull, lifeless geeks who only understand ones and zeros. No. It *celebrates* it. It turns it into the central message. It plays with the concept and has no end of fun with it. More importantly, though, while it celebrates the engineer stereotype, at the same time it smashes it to pieces.

Engineers make buying decisions on emotion no differently than the rest of us do. Storytelling *does* work when marketing to them, no differently than people in any other profession. Plus, every geek out there has suffered the heartache of unrequited love.

Every time Mike sends out an e-mail blast, he gets e-mails back from customers saying "Your newsletter is the only one I read every time it comes" and "I always look forward to getting e-mails from you guys."

WHY WE CHOSE ENGINEERS AS AN EXAMPLE FOR E-MAIL MARKETING

Most people stubbornly insist that you can't use storytelling and humor to sell to "logical" people like engineers and scientists. Most people also think that B2B marketing has to be dreadfully serious.

Well, this example shoots holes in both beliefs. We're doing both at the same time here—using emotional, human-touch e-mail marketing to sell B2B products to engineers and scientists.

Does this work in other markets? You bet it does. Bryan has sold more books on learning Chinese and ignited more feedback and fan mail through this one message than anything else he sends out:

Subject: **WOMEN WHO HOLD HANDS; MEN WHO HUG**

William kept brushing against me as we walked down the street.

Now I'm a guy like he is—and I'm straight, too—and I found this a little unnerving. This was back during my first month living in mainland China, William was my new friend, and he had some habits that were awfully strange.

And when we'd go out walking somewhere, he always rubbed his shoulders up against me. I kept thinking I was crowding him, so I'd move to the right. Then he'd move right too, get closer and rub up against me again.

Sooner or later I figured out that this was just his way of being friendly. No, not "friendly," just friendly—you know, normal, nice-guy friendly.

It's that classic issue of personal space. Every culture has different rules. My Chinese guy friends rubbed shoulders with each other,

and with me, as they walked down the street.
Americans don't do that, unless they're in a
relationship.

Younger women in China hold hands.
Sometimes regardless of age. Arm in arm, hand
in hand, they saunter together down the street.

Ah, but do they HUG you?

None of my friends ever did.

At least, not until I was with a couple of
guys being visited by a lady pal of theirs from
Shanghai . . . .

This e-mail is part of Bryan's regular autoresponder, and it doesn't even explicitly promote his book. But it gets a *reaction* from people. It turns the spotlight in a sensitive yet eminently funny subject.

It paints Bryan as completely and totally human. Not a peddler, not a salesman, not a pushy marketer, but as a regular guy whose experiences his mainland readers all share.

Most importantly, he *trains* people to read his e-mails by convincing them that he's always got something interesting to say.

4. People Can't Forget You When They Hear from You Often

Get an autoresponder series going, and you can win the hearts of customers for life:

1. We like five-day sequences. Five is a good number. Prime numbers like 3, 5, and 7 are good.
2. After that five-day sequence is done, keep in touch at a slower rate. In our "Nine Great Lies of Sales & Marketing" e-course (www.PerryMarshall .com/9), messages continue every few days and taper out for more than two years afterward. (You read it right, two years.)
3. Your unsubscribe rate should be 3 to 10 percent. If it's more than that, your message isn't matching your market. If it's less, congratulations.

4. Want to squash refunds and returns? After someone buys from you, send them a series of messages that shows them how to use your product more effectively and share features they might have missed. When we do this, it cuts returns by half or more.

5. When people complain that they've missed a day or two from you, it's a sign that your content is good *and* that the spam filters are doing their job.

5. If You Violate the Expectation of Relevance, You Damage Your List

Let's say you're a chiropractor and you've just launched a new herbal remedy. It's a fantastic product, and you want to tell your customers. What should you do? Should you blast your entire list with it? Odds are, you could maximize your sales total for that day by doing so.

But you're going to pay a price. All the people on your list who aren't interested in herbal stuff are now going to be *less responsive* to everything else you do, even if they don't unsubscribe. You've just taught them that you like to send out e-mails about stuff they're not interested in. That means they're that much less likely to read your next e-mail.

It's a nasty mistake to treat everyone on your list in the same way unless they really are. If you've got a back pain newsletter, it's likely only a few people on that list would ever be interested in a knee pain newsletter.

The typical marketer will treat everyone in the same way, and when he gets a back pain subscriber, he'll also send knee pain stuff, neck pain stuff, herbal stuff, environmental stuff, whatever. The smart marketer will not. The smart marketer will have different lists for each topic—different sublists.

So if you're the chiropractor, you build an herbal sublist, and then sell the herbal remedies just to those folks. That way you maximize the value of every single list you have.

In e-mail, and by extension, direct mail and other forms of communication, that means that some of your prospects and customers don't ever want to hear from you (the bottom 5 to 10 percent). They, of course, do not matter. They can unsubscribe. But for the people who do:

- Some of them, maybe 50 percent, would like to hear from you no more than a few times a year.

- Some of them (20 percent) would like to get your three-, five-, or seven-day autoresponder sequence for a few days, then only hear from you if something really important happens.
- Some, 5 to 10 percent, would like to get all your newsletters, and if you have e-mail lists for six different problems or products, they'll want to be on every single one.
- Some, 1 to 2 percent, would like to hear from you every day.
- A tiny handful, less than 1 percent, would literally read ten e-mails from you every day, if you were willing to send them.

6. The Human Touch Sells

Don't hide behind your e-mail. Use it to express more of yourself. You're not a faceless corporation; you're a person. Show that side of you, and people will remember you. And buy. And tell others about you.

Express a personality that people can instantly recognize. This is free branding. When you introduce new products or make changes in your marketing program or message, now you can attach those to a name, your name or another person that your business is known for, and now your name itself has even more meaning and credibility.

PAY FOR E-MAIL—NOT A PROBLEM

As of this writing, AOL, Yahoo, and others are in the late stages of a system for paid e-mail. In order to send large numbers of messages to AOL or Yahoo users, you will have to pay one cent or a fraction of a cent each to get your messages through.

E-mail has been free for years, but according to the natural order of things, it shouldn't be. It's been free simply because ISPs haven't had a uniform standard system for taking payment and authenticating legitimate senders' addresses. But they're getting there, and fast.

Information all over the internet was once accessible for free, but then memberships and payment services began to clean that up. Just as clicks used to be either by-impression only or free, now they're not. Information is worth money.

Rumors of paid e-mail have been circulating for years, but the internet service providers are closing in on agreed-upon standards. It's just like HDTV, which has literally been talked about for decades, but has come to fruition only in the last couple of years.

There is no free lunch. ISPs stay in business with free e-mail now only by making it a front-end free entry to later back-end offers, publicity, and advertising opportunities. But e-mail like everything else *will* start coming at a price.

This is not an apocalypse; it's something to embrace. It means that your customers' inboxes will be far less cluttered than they are now. Because e-mails now have to justify their existence by being cost-effective, the quality of messages can only go up. It also means that if you have a lengthy autoresponder series that you're sending out to your customers, you'll now be adding those few extra cents to the cost of acquiring each of those customers.

Your job will be tougher, but when you make it succeed, your marketing machine will be leaner, meaner, more effective. The quality and value of your e-mail list will go *up,* not down.

DIRECT MAIL ALL OVER AGAIN

The more things change, the more they stay the same. E-mail is coming into its own now. It's an electronic version of what direct mail has been for over a hundred years.

Marketers who have built their entire businesses on the blissful assumption that e-mail is forever free will have reality to reckon with. Direct mail costs you postage, plus materials. E-mails will have their own postage costs as well, and that will clean up the clutter of our inboxes.

You're better off going offline in your marketing *now.* Communicating with your customers via direct mail or fax takes you out of the ephemeral, fly-by-night online world and plugs them into you by an entirely new medium, a medium that is harder to break into but potentially more rewarding and enduring.

You can bank on the fact that the guy in the blue-gray uniform who comes to your house every day is going to *continue* coming to your house every day pretty much as long as the earth keeps rotating on its axis. A customer who finds you offline and goes to you online is usually more valuable to you than a customer who knows you only online. In the same way, a customer who knows you offline through physical mailings and physical products as well as online is going to be a much more valuable customer than one who only knows you online.

OPT-INS: MORE THAN JUST AN E-MAIL ADDRESS?

Most opt-in pages only ask for a name and e-mail address, but is that all the information you want? Many, if not most, businesses should also collect physical addresses and fax numbers. Asking for this information, even requiring it, makes your database much more valuable. It also gives you a valuable communication medium besides just e-mail. What if you accidentally get on a spam blacklist, your e-mail service goes belly up, or e-mail suddenly gets a lot more expensive? It's a mistake to rely solely on e-mail.

THEY CAN KNOCK OFF YOUR PRODUCT, BUT THEY CAN'T KNOCK OFF *YOU*

Anybody can have a TV talk show, but there's only one Oprah. Anybody can rant about the Democrats, but there's only one Rush Limbaugh. Products can be replicated and ideas can be stolen, but personalities cannot be duplicated. Use e-mail to express your own personality and you'll have a unique bond with your customers that nobody can take from you.

Uncle Claude Sez

To create the right individuality is a supreme accomplishment. Then an advertiser's growing reputation on that line brings him ever-increasing prestige. Never weary of that part.

That's why we have signed ads sometimes—to give them a personal authority. A man is talking—a man who takes pride in his accomplishments—not a "soulless corporation." Whenever possible we introduce a personality into our ads. By making a man famous we make his product famous. When we claim an improvement, naming the man who made it adds effect.

CHAPTER 13

The Winning Method the World's Smartest Marketers Stole from the Wright Brothers

The boneyard of modern civilization is littered with "great" marketing ideas that never got off the ground. Think of the billions and trillions of dollars that companies spend developing products, only to find out that their products aren't what people wanted in the first place.

■ ■ ■

Let's *not* assume you're a corporation with billions of dollars to spend. Instead, let's assume you're a regular guy who quit a cushy job to pursue an entrepreneurial vision. As you calculate it, you've got to start making a profit in six to nine months or else you'll run out of money.

If that's you, then you can't afford to make a mistake. You can't spend three months developing a product and later find out in month six that the product has to be totally redesigned. That'll kill your business and send you back to the J.O.B. with your tail between your legs.

We're going to make sure this never happens to you.

How can you prevent this? By testing your product idea and even your web site itself on the cheap, using Google, *before* you've spent a lot of money on it. With the internet, you can find out if a product idea will succeed or fail, for a few hundred to no more than a few thousand dollars. If you do this, you will be sure that the product you develop will be well received.

HOW THE WRIGHT BROTHERS' SAVVY TESTING METHOD MADE THEM FIRST IN FLIGHT

The year: 1903. The place: a houseboat on the Potomac River, USA. Just weeks before Wilbur and Orville Wright were to fly the world's first airplane at Kitty Hawk, North Carolina, Samuel Pierpont Langley, a well-funded engineer and inventor, was launching an airplane of his own—with the assistance of an entire staff.

Langley's assumption: Put a big enough engine on the thing, and it will fly. He focused all his effort on that one project: creating an engine powerful enough for the plane to go airborne. On October 7th, 1903, Langley tested his model for the very first time. *The plane crashed immediately after leaving the launch pad, badly damaging the front wing.*

Two months later, just eight days before the Wright Brothers' successful flight, Langley made a second attempt. *This time the tail and rear wing collapsed completely during launch.*

Langley was ridiculed by the press and criticized by members of the Congress for throwing away taxpayer dollars on his failed projects. (Can you imagine the cynicism? Some sneering reporters were sure that nobody could or would ever fly.) Disillusioned by the public response, Langley abandoned his vision.

Wilbur and Orville Wright, meanwhile, had a completely different approach: build a glider that would glide from a hilltop with no engine at all. They focused their energy on balance and steering. Power was almost an afterthought. Only after the glider worked by itself would they try to put an engine on it.

After three years of tedious experimentation, the glider was working well, so they commissioned bicycle shop machinist Charlie Taylor to build them an engine. It was the smallest engine he could design—a 12-horsepower unit that weighed 180 pounds. *And on December 17, 1903, at Kitty Hawk, North Carolina, Wilbur and Orville Wright made history.*

The Wright Brothers changed the world and became famous historical figures, whereas few have ever heard of Langley. Their approach of making the plane fly *before* applying high power was the winning idea.

> *Langley had spent most of four years building an extraordinary engine to lift their heavy flying machine. The Wrights had spent most of four years building a flying machine so artfully designed that it could be propelled into the air by a fairly ordinary internal combustion engine.*
>
> —SMITHSONIAN MAGAZINE, APRIL 2003

> *Skill comes by the constant repetition of familiar feats rather than by a few overbold attempts at feats for which the performer is yet poorly prepared.*
>
> —WILBUR WRIGHT

Samuel Pierpont Langley died in 1906, a broken and disappointed man.

THOSE WHO TEST, FLY. THOSE WHO RELY ON BRUTE FORCE, DIE.

You don't want to die a broke and disappointed man or woman. You want to die rich and famous. Right? Then there is a direct comparison between the Wright Brothers and your career as an internet marketer.

The search engine is the motor. Your web site is the glider. A motor without a good set of wings does you no good. When you put an engine on a glider, you have a plane. When you feed traffic to a web site that can "fly," you have a business.

And as smart marketers like Uncle Claude have known for over a century, you get the wings to work through careful, systematic testing. This is not a new concept. For more than a hundred years, smart, savvy marketers have followed these time-tested principles of proven good sense and made their dollars go many times further.

In 1923, Uncle Claude said:

> *Advertising and merchandising become exact sciences. Every course is charted. The compass of accurate knowledge directs the shortest, safest, cheapest course to any destination.*
>
> *We learn the principles and prove them by repeated tests . . . . We compare one way with many others, backward and forwards, and record the results.*

Advertising is traced down to the fraction of a penny. The cost per reply and cost per dollar of sale show up with utter exactness.

One ad compared to another, one method with another. Headlines, settings, sizes, arguments and pictures are compared. To reduce the cost of results even one per cent means much.

So no guesswork is permitted. One must know what is best.

Building a business online doesn't have to be guesswork. It's not a crapshoot. It's a *science*. Wise men and women before us have taken the risks, tested the limits, learned the hard lessons for us, and laid down a clear path that we can follow with confidence.

Whether your business is all online, or only partly so, the foundation remains the same: Start small, test carefully, make modest improvements, get deeper insights into your market, test some more, and you'll *know* that your business is going to grow.

This well-worn path builds a sales process that works. When you have a persuasive web site, you have a glider. Just like the Wright Brothers, all you need to do is put a lightweight engine on it and you can fly.

Add Google traffic the smart way, and you've got a business that soars. *Google AdWords can bring you a lot of traffic, and that traffic is valuable to the extent that your web site can convert the traffic to leads and sales.* When you're getting started, Google is like a lightweight engine that you can turn on and off instantly. You can test your glider safely without crashing, killing a potential joint venture partnership, or blowing a wad of money.

MARKETING MISERY IS *NOT* NECESSARY

Thousands of people go to bed every night wondering *why? Why can't I make any sales? Why can't I earn any real money at this?*

Consider the dotcom boom in 1997–2000. The players were a lot like Langley. They focused on the engine instead of the wings. When it didn't take off, they just poured more gas into the engine. When that didn't work, they put it on a rocket launcher and forced it up into the air.

You don't have the time or the money to pour into product ideas and sales messages that, in hindsight, were "almost right." Your spouse won't let you blow the grocery money or college savings on a lark.

Reality is a great teacher, if you let it speak its piece. The people who click on your ads will tell you what they want, if you ask them. They'll show you what they want, if you watch them.

Uncle Claude Sez

The time has come when advertising has in some hands reached the status of a science. It is based on fixed principles and is reasonably exact. The causes and effects have been analyzed until they are well understood.

The correct methods of procedure have been proved and established. We know what is most effective, and we act on basic law.

Advertising, once a gamble, has thus become, under able direction, one of the safest business ventures.

Certainly no other enterprise with comparable possibilities need involve so little risk.

Therefore, this book deals, not with theories and opinions, but with well-proven principles and facts. It is written as a text book for students and a safe guide for advertisers. Every statement has been weighed.

Get Customers to Eat Out of Your Hand

Marketing history is littered with spectacular product launch failures. The most famous one of all time may be Ford's Edsel, but there are countless others, most of which die a quiet death. Nobody ever hears about them. Every product launch failure consumes time, money, and resources that could have—or would have—launched a successful product. If your product launch fails, you lose twice. And while you can never purge all the risk out of new projects, you can use Google traffic and survey data to get a sanity check, and sometimes quite inexpensively.

■ ■ ■

Next time you roll out a new product, you can have a 75 percent or better chance of success by using Google to measure your traffic. You can know exactly how much demand there is for your idea. You can test your headlines and copy and have your potential customers tell you exactly what kind of product they're looking for. Google makes this far less expensive and far less risky than ever before.

WE USED GOOGLE ADWORDS TO PICK A TITLE FOR A SEMINAR

Do you know what's wrong with most market research? It's not market research, it's opinion research. Opinions are what people *say*. Markets are about what people *do*.

In his landmark book *Blink: The Power of Thinking without Thinking* (Little Brown, 2005), author Malcolm Gladwell talks about this: People's buying decisions are usually an impulse act, and the reasons they *tell* you after the fact for buying a certain item or liking a particular product may have nothing whatsoever to do with their real reason.

Focus groups won't tell you the real reason. In-depth surveys won't get to the bottom of it. Often the only way to know what attracts customers is to give options and let them act in real time. Then go with what works, even when you don't know their personal reasons why. Here's one such example of powerful, real-time market research on the internet.

How Google Quickly Assessed the Viability of an Event Name

I'm the marketing and publicity director of TruthQuest, which is a local nonprofit group that hosts speakers and discussions on a variety of hot topics in religion and theology. After the smash success of *Lord of the Rings,* its sequel, *The Two Towers* followed the next winter. We found ourselves a speaker, Professor Jerry Root of Wheaton College, who could talk about this movie and the philosophical point of view of its author, J.R.R. Tolkien.

No matter how great the speaker may be, it doesn't matter if nobody shows up. So the title of the event was crucial. Somebody suggested a preliminary title: "Is *Lord of the Rings* Christian?" I didn't like it. Not intriguing. Too easy to say "No" or "Yes" and forget about it.

The more marketing I do, the less I trust myself even to pick a good title. So our group brainstormed four titles, and let the world vote on them. I used Google AdWords and had an answer in just 18 hours.

What Happened When We Ran the Overnight Test

I took our proposed titles and made four ads, all rotating simultaneously. I purchased the keyword "Tolkien," as well as "Tolkein," a common misspelling that people often mistakenly search on.

(Clickthroughs on misspelled words are often two to three times as high, and the words are less expensive because there are so many other vendors who aren't bidding on them. *Yet one out of every seven searches misspells the name "Tolkien"!)*

I started running the ad on Google at about 3:00 P.M. on a weekday and stopped it at 8:00 A.M. the next morning. Here's what the ads looked like, along with their results:

The Two Towers
Tolkien, The Two Towers, and
Spiritual Symbolism
tolkiensociety.org

11 Clicks | 1.0% CTR | $0.06 CPC

Spirituality of Tolkien
Hidden Messages in
The Two Towers
tolkiensociety.org

20 Clicks | 1.9% CTR | $0.05 CPC

Lord Of The Rings
and The Spiritual Powers
of Hobbits
tolkiensociety.org

8 Clicks | 0.7% CTR | $0.06 CPC

Tolkien Spirituality
Is There Hidden Christianity
In The Two Towers?
tolkiensociety.org

16 Clicks | 1.5% CTR | $0.06 CPC

Keyword	Clicks	Impressions	CTR	Cost
tolkien	**48**	3878	**1.2%**	$2.43
tolkein	7	252	**2.7%**	$0.35
Overall	**55**	4130	**1.3%**	$2.78

What We Found Out

As you can see, clickthrough rates were dramatically different for different titles. The winner was "Spirituality of Tolkien: Hidden Messages in the Two Towers." This was *vastly* better than doing a focus group or a survey of our friends. Why? Because when someone reads about this in the newspaper or on a flier, their decision either to continue reading or to ignore it is made *on impulse.* They don't sit and ponder it. The decision to click on a link is equally impulsive.

This is a *great* way to come up with titles for magazine articles, white papers, books, and names for new products. And believe me, the votes you get will surprise you. What you *think* sounds cool is probably not what your customers think is relevant.

You can use this exact method to test the marketability of almost *any* idea you have. You can take it a step further than I did, bringing visitors to your own web site and further testing their response to different offers.

HOW TO BE SURE THERE'S A MORE PROFITABLE MARKET FOR YOUR IDEA

By developing a product after your customers tell you what they want, you can have a product for which there is demand. Let's say you're thinking about writing a software program for doing automotive repairs. It's for do-it-yourself car enthusiasts and does engine diagnostics that help increase fuel efficiency by five miles per gallon.

If a guy bought your software (which you haven't written yet), he could buy a cable at Radio Shack, take his computer into his garage, hook it up to his car, and the software would collect a load of data and display it on the screen. Your program would then tell the guy what to tweak in his engine.

Sounds like a great idea. But how do you know there's a market for this? You can find out if there's water in the swimming pool before you dive in. You certainly don't want to spend months writing software if nobody's going to buy it. So here's what you do:

1. *Write an e-book, white paper or guide.* Call it "How to Use Engine Diagnostics to Improve Your Car's Fuel Efficiency by Five Miles per Gallon." In it you tell people how to do it the *hard way*, the whole routine that takes you three days, including the spreadsheet and the connector from Radio Shack. (I have a free e-mail course on writing white papers at www.perrymar shall.com/whitepapers.)

2. *Head for Google and bid on starter keywords.* Find all of the major terms related to engine diagnostics.

3. *Post an ad.*

DIY Engine Diagnostics

Simple Procedure Improves
Your Car—5 MPG or Better
www.AutoDiag.com

On your landing page, you have a sales letter that tells them about your e-book. You can also follow up with a series of e-mails that talk more about this.

4. *Get ideas and feedback from your readers.*

5. *Sell the e-book.* Or even give it away for free. But not without a plan. While you're marketing your e-book, you're going to take the next step with your buyers.

6. *Test your customers' response to your actual product idea.* What do they say back to you? Are they interested? Do they pester you to find out when this will be available? Do they offer to pay you for it now, hoping to get first dibs on it when it comes out? If so, you know you've got a winner.

7. *Sell your product.* The dollars will come rolling in.

You've listened to your customers; you've put together a product in line with what they ask you for; you've proven to yourself that they're interested. Now when you give them exactly what they want, you'll make the cash register ring.

WHAT YOU LEARN WHEN YOUR IDEA DOESN'T WORK THE FIRST TIME

Now what happens if it's a flop? Don't cry in your milk. Learn your lesson and get on with something else. You can come up with a new idea and test it for no great sum of money.

And what if the idea is only marginal? *Play with it.* Change your ad, change your landing page, fiddle with the title of your report or e-book, adjust the price if you sell it, give visitors incentives in exchange for lots of feedback, and try again. If it won't work, then move on. If you can clear out the bugs, then run like the wind.

Did you know that infomercials also run on this same premise? It costs $50,000 to $100,000 to produce an infomercial and run it for a few days. If the producer can get 80 percent return on investment (i.e., only lose 20 percent) the first time out, he won't scrap the project. He'll play with the offer, the upsells, the testimonials, and the other ingredients until he gets it above break-even. And he's not afraid to cut his losses if he has to.

When you test ideas that don't work, *fail fast.* Get it over with as quickly as possible. Spend the money, get the results, cut your losses, and move on.

"Wait a minute," you might be thinking, "I don't have hundreds of dollars to blow on pre-testing. I can't afford to do that." The reality is, you can't afford *not* to. Spending those dollars and going into the red now could save you *thousands* of dollars later in botched advertising and mediocre returns, and can prevent you from having to start again from scratch.

The Insights You Get When Customers Vomit All Over You

I spent more than four years in mainland China, during which time I went from not even knowing how to say "hello" to becoming conversationally fluent in the language. It saddened me as I watched many of my Western friends there struggling with the language and getting nowhere.

Through trial and error I learned a host of practical, working methods for acquiring the language. Multiple times during my stay there my American and European friends would tell me, "Wow, you need to share your whole method with me, because whatever it is, it's obviously working."

So I listened. And after returning to the United States, I sat down to write a book that would teach other English speakers to do just what I did.

I then decided to take our marketing advice: I wrote a series of autoresponder e-mails and bought Google traffic *first*, planning to sell the book to customers later.

I set up my Google campaign, sent traffic to my new web site, www.Master ChineseFaster.com, and let it go.

Here are two of the responses I got:

> *You have shown me absolutely nothing. You have wasted my time and paper printing off your worthless e-mails. I learned more in five minutes from a Chinese business web site than I could ever expect to learn from your time-wasting activities.*
>
> —D.M.

> *You have not provided me with any practice Mandarin lessons, which is what I wanted. Instead you provided generic information, as a "carrot" to buy your course. This is a scam.*
>
> —F.P.

Oh, crap! Here I am in the middle of writing a book about learning the language living in China, while these people are in their home country looking for simple online lessons. Thank God I hadn't created a whole product yet.

But get this: they *did* tell me exactly what they were looking for. The first guy above left me the URL of the Chinese business site he had mentioned, so I could go and compare. The second guy told me specifically that he wanted "practice Mandarin lessons." Others weighed in, too.

These people wanted online lessons. I didn't have the resources to put something like that together at the time. But I logged it away to pursue in the future.

Now what about my e-book? Should I cancel the project? No. I *knew* from experience with friends that I had something of tremendous value. But how was I going to find the folks who really needed it?

I finished the book and set my ads to show only in Taiwan and Mainland China, and not even in Hong Kong, where Cantonese and English are more common than Mandarin. I turned on the traffic again.

When Your Machine Finally Kicks In

That's when the positive e-mails started pouring in. Grateful readers who had moved to China and Taiwan from the United States, Israel, Germany, Australia, the United Kingdom, New Zealand, India, indeed, all over the globe, wrote in to tell me that they were finding my e-mail course helpful and relevant.

More importantly, *they were buying the book* and telling me that they were using it. I even found myself doing late-night telephone consultations to Beijing with my customers, helping them improve their Chinese-learning strategy even further.

In reality, the book is an invaluable resource regardless of what language a person is learning. The principles are universal and apply anywhere in the world. Still, focusing on China and Taiwan paid off.

One buyer sent me this:

> *At about midnight last night, I paid for and downloaded your products. I thought I would take a quick glance before going to bed.*
>
> *It is now five o'clock on Sunday afternoon, and I haven't been to bed yet. I read the entire document twice; your bonus article three times. During this time, I experienced a gamut of emotions; everything from the knowing smile, kissing the computer screen, wildly punching the air, and dancing around the room.*
>
> *Your product is excellent, Bryan, and worth every cent I paid for it. For the price, I could not have had a better night! Don't even think about returning my money, as I love your work, and I am looking forward to any stuff you do in the future.*
>
> —ANDREW V.

When you find your market, *boy, do you ever find them!* Giving people exactly what they need and then having them turn around and thank you for it is the true joy of marketing. The market has spoken. The book is selling. I'm making a profit. People like Andrew are writing testimonials, which in turn sells more books.

My customers keep telling me they want actual learning materials and the actual experience of studying with a person. So I'm hard at work now, putting together a unique international Chinese learning program that incorporates the principles that I already teach.

WHEN YOUR MARKET SPEAKS AND YOU RESPOND, IT'S MONEY IN THE BANK

Start small with Google, and when your market talks, listen. You'll knock your head against a few walls in the early going, but there's no better education to be had. Behind every angry rant you hear is someone who didn't get what they really wanted. Go with what your prospects tell you they want. And don't ever stop asking. Especially when your *existing customers* talk. That's as good as money in the bank.

Since I lived in China for four years, I listened for *four years* as friends and acquaintances complained about their struggles in learning the language. That taught me *what* I need to create for people. Then I spent two weeks listening to my Google visitors in order to discover *where* I needed to market it.

Then Andrew used the book. It improved his Chinese. He wrote back to tell me about it. His testimonial resulted in more sales. He went on and told friends and coworkers. Word traveled around. More people bought.

That's exactly what people will do for you when you hit their sweet spot.

Uncle Claude Sez

Almost any questions can be answered, cheaply, quickly and finally, by a test campaign. That is the way to answer them, not by arguments around a table. Go to the court of last resort: the buyers of your product . . . .

We establish averages on a small scale, and those averages always hold. We know our cost, we know our sale, and we know our profit and loss. We know how soon our cost comes back. Before we spread out, we prove our undertaking absolutely safe.

Converting Visitors to Buyers

T
he internet is instantaneous: give people what they want the instant they crave it. Otherwise they'll spend their money with your competitor.

■ ■ ■

Here's a way to think of this: If you sell California White Water Rafting trips, and someone searches "California white water rafting" then your ad should exactly match her search, and the page she lands on should continue with that thought. It should be so smooth and natural that the easiest thing for her to do is go ahead and enter her credit card information and book the trip, because she doesn't want to go back to Google and look for something else.

That's how you keep your visitors from getting frustrated with your site and get them to buy from you instead of someone else.

We got an e-mail with the following rant:

> Why can't people just give me what I want?
>
> I went searching for "hedge funds" yesterday. Only *one* of the AdWords ads had that exact phrase in it (only one—imagine that!) so I clicked. The ad had made it look like I would get some very clear directives on how to learn more.
>
> But no. The ad took me to some stupid corporate home page, which had no hedge fund information whatsoever. I went clicking around the site. Still nothing. I finally gave up and went and did something else.
>
> *I want to know more about hedge funds!* For crying out loud, I'm ready to *pay money* to learn this stuff. Why can't these corporate idiot web designers figure that out?

This is so common it's not funny. If millions of people are searching for what I've got, why would I set up a site, buy clicks, and then not give them exactly what they're looking for?

Maybe those hedge fund experts figure that guys surfing the web will just call them on the phone. *Wrong!* They could have given him what he was looking for, *and* collected his contact information, and stayed in touch with him for months afterward. He was ready to do business. They weren't. So he left, money in hand.

THE SINGLE BIGGEST WEB SITE MISTAKE MARKETERS MAKE

When your AdWords ad leads perfectly to a landing page that gives people what they want and provokes action, you've got a winning ad campaign. It's a very simple formula.

For example, I have a book that I sell online that teaches people how to master Mandarin Chinese more quickly. It's ideal for English speakers living in mainland China or Taiwan. So I post this Google ad:

Want to Learn Chinese?
5 Crucial Principles You Must Know
To Master Chinese, and Fast
MasterChineseFaster.com

It takes people to this landing page where they can read about my five-day course that teaches these five principles, and sign up right there:

On many days, a 30 percent signup rate for my e-course is not uncommon.

This principle works again and again, no matter what your market. Tell people exactly what you're going to give them, and deliver immediately.

Uncle Claude Sez

Remember the people you address are selfish, as we all are. They care nothing about your interests or your profit. They seek service for themselves. Ignoring this fact is a common mistake and a costly mistake in advertising. Ads say in effect, "Buy my brand. Give me the trade you give to others. Let me have the money."

That is not a popular appeal.

The best ads ask no one to buy. That is useless. Often they do not quote a price. They do not say that dealers handle the product.

The ads are based entirely on service. They offer wanted information. They site advantages to users. Perhaps they offer a sample, or to buy the first package, or to send something on approval, so the customer may prove the claims without any cost or risks. Some of these ads seem altruistic. But they are based on the knowledge of human nature. The writers know how people are led to buy.

Here again is salesmanship. The good salesman does not merely cry a name. He doesn't say, "Buy my article." He pictures the customer's side of his service until the natural result is to buy.

CHAPTER 16

Google's Conversion Tracking Tells You What's Working

You're a smart Google user when you know your numbers: How much each click is worth, what you can afford to spend to get a customer, and the Return on Investment for each ingredient in your AdWords mix. This is a well-oiled machine that can generate profit for you night and day for years.

■ ■ ■

Josh was burning up the pages on Google. He had a fine-tuned herbal supplements AdWords campaign that was breaking new CTR records literally every week. Traffic was screaming. Product was moving. People were buying. Dollars were changing hands.

But then the credit card statements came in. Josh compared his credit card statement from Google with his sales reports. *The ship was leaking!* He was losing money, lots of it, fast. The left hand didn't know what the right hand was doing. He had no tracking system set up. No way to trace sales back to clicks, no way to know where to plug the leaks.

Josh called us in a panic. So we went over to www.Hypertracker.net and set him up with an account there. He tracked every sales dollar back to the ad group it came from. He had put in place a system that was lean, mean, dirty. Every penny going out accounted for. Every dollar coming in measured for profit down to the cent.

With this newfound knowledge Josh beefed up his Google advertising even more, trimmed off the fat, and in a ferociously competitive herbal supplement market (where new competitors show up daily and soon drop off like flies), he went on to solid profitability.

Now Josh can take his supplements business wherever he wants. He can reinvest his profit and expand, or he can put it on autopilot and pursue other ventures. Josh has succeeded because he keeps close tabs on every number, all the time.

WASTED CORPORATE ADVERTISING DOLLARS VS. YOUR PROFIT-GENERATING TRAFFIC MACHINE

If you called up your stockbroker and asked him, "How much is IBM selling for today?" what would you think if he mumbled, "Oh, IBM's been fine" and dodged the rest of your questions? You'd get a new stockbroker! You want to know exactly how much your stock is worth, in dollars and cents. That's the only way you know if you're making money or not.

The same applies to the operation of any aspect of your business: your web site, your mailings, your employees, your phone and utilities, everything. You may have heard people say, "I know that half of my advertising dollars are wasted; I just don't know which half." If you were Coca-Cola and you did image advertising on a mass-marketed consumer product, that might be the hard reality of things. But you're not Coca-Cola. You can do far better.

The mail order business has known this secret for decades: *One really good ad in the right place can make money for you month after month for years, with no changes or alterations.* That's because when you use rigorous methods to identify advertising formulas that work, you're going to do as much of it as you possibly can. More, if you're in a recession. If advertising is the great hidden waste in corporate America, effective results-accountable advertising is one of the great secrets of small business success.

Business has never been better for us because we incorporated tracking mechanisms a long time ago. We can glance at a few numbers and see where we're at. We teach our clients how to succeed in marketing themselves and their businesses the exact same way we market ourselves and our business.

You can track your own Google clicks and advertising dollars using the same systems, the same mechanisms, the same techniques, and the same criteria that we use.

SET UP GOOGLE TRACKING TO PERFECT YOUR ADS AND GROW YOUR BUSINESS EVEN MORE

Google makes it kindergarten simple for you to track your conversions and sales all the way back to every keyword in your list. You can turn up traffic where it's the most profitable for you and trim back dollars where they're being wasted. *Tracking clicks to sales is not optional, by the way; it's mandatory if you want to get all the profit that's available to you.* In competitive markets, it's the only way to survive.

There's a host of conversion programs and subscription services you can buy that do conversion tracking, split testing of landing pages and sales letters, web analytics, and more. In general, if you're giving Google your money, it's better to give somebody else the job of reporting your results. However, Google's tracking is effective, and it's integrated with the AdWords system itself.

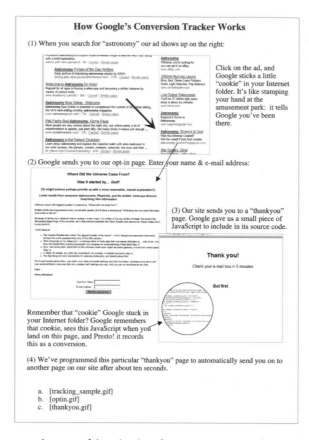

Google's conversion tracking is simple to set up. On the toolbar at the top of your campaign summary page, click on "Conversion Tracking," and Google will give you the options for which type of action you want to track:

From there you can generate a simple piece of javascript that you'll stick in the code of your Thank You page where the only people who see it are the ones who have signed up or made a purchase:

Now as people opt in to your site, or as they buy, Google will tell you how well you're turning clicks into sales or actions, and which keywords generate conversions better than the others.

Even better still, you can tell which *ads* you're writing are turning into more conversions and which ones aren't. To see this, click on the "Reports" tab up at the top and select "Text ad performance" from the drop-down menu:

Want to make your engine hum? This is where you tweak and test more, and hone your advertising to perfection:

- You can bid more on keywords that are highly profitable, and get even more good traffic from them.
- You can delete irrelevant keywords that are wasting your money.
- You can trim spending on ad groups and campaigns that have thin margins.
- You can identify whether content-targeted advertising is making you money, or losing it.
- You can spot which sites you're advertising on that are bringing in the most cash.
- You can tell which ads are attracting more paying customers.

This is where the profit is in Google AdWords!

QUICK EXAMPLE OF CONVERSION TRACKING

Here's a pair of keywords that showed up in the same ad campaign. Both bid at the same price. Both ran off of the same ads. But I knew I had a limit where I could not go over $1.10 cost per conversion; otherwise it would be losing me money. One succeeded, one didn't. So I deleted the keyword that didn't:

And here's a Google report on two ads that ran in the same ad group. They both sent traffic to the same page and were both triggered by the same keywords at the same bid price. Oddly enough, their CTR was identical—0.3 percent. But one converted 30 percent of the visitors to leads, while the other converted only 13 percent. And the cost per lead of the second one was nearly double. One came out the winner, and one was the loser. So I deleted the loser:

When I did this, I made more money the following month. Google gave me the information I needed to streamline my marketing engine even more.

OUTSMART THE LAW OF DIMINISHING RETURNS

If you've got keywords that are doing screamingly well, do you just up the bid price on them and aim for the top positions on the page? It sounds logical, but experience sometimes tells otherwise. The more you pay, the worse your traffic may get. Don't assume that you'll make the most money by being in the top positions. Very often, the opposite is true: you'll *lose* the most money by being in the top positions because of 1) the price you pay to get into those positions, and 2) the low quality traffic that you'll get from them.

One of our clients, John Jaworski of X-Streamers, sells confetti and party supplies for large events and venues. He was doing conversion tracking just like we've described here, and words like "party confetti" and "wedding confetti" were doing just fine. But he was paying $0.65 per click for a high-ranking position on "confetti" and had gotten 1,200 visitors—with zero sales.

Some people would consider $0.65 cheap. Compared to the $10 and $20 prices you pay for keywords in some markets, that's a bargain. Nevertheless, we advised John to cut his bid price by 90 percent and get his listing on page *two* of the search results instead of page one. He dropped his bid to $0.07.

You might think that would have killed his traffic and sales. Amazingly, the opposite happened: his traffic started *seriously* converting!

This is not unusual, and for big-market, high-traffic categories (i.e., the top few hundred most searched terms on the web) even the page-two and page-three listings can get you decent amounts of traffic.

Real savings and money well spent come in finding that "sweet spot" between paying a *low price* for clicks (which generally improves the conversion rate) and still getting a *good position* (which increases your traffic). You have direct control over this because you set the price. And as you watch your campaigns over time, you can move that CPC up or down to hit the perfect middle ground between price and position.

You'll know you've hit that "sweet spot" when your net profit is the highest. This is something you can set and tweak individually for literally every single keyword in your entire account. (Realistically you only need to do this for the top 10 to 30 individual keywords, which for most people will represent 95 percent of the traffic.)

ADSENSE AND CONTENT-TARGETED TRAFFIC

AdSense is Google's program that lets site owners display syndicated Google AdWords ads on their sites and earn a few extra cents of their own each time visitors click through. Unlike regular search engine traffic where ads show based solely on the keywords you typed in, AdSense ads are *content-targeted*, i.e., Google shows them based on the content of the page and of the site. Here are ads shown when you search on an online dictionary for "migraine."

Rather than appearing on sites like AOL or Earthlink, content-targeted advertising puts your ads on sites like Dictionary.com, Amazon.com, the *Los Angeles Times* web site, and so on.

Making money as an AdSense partner and putting Google ads on your web site is a whole 'nother topic for another book. This section is about how to take advantage of this option if you're the advertiser.

You can opt to turn content-targeted traffic on or off, so that your ads either show on sites like these or they don't. A more recent option that Google has made available is Site-Targeted AdSense, where you can pay per-impression rather than per-click, and choose which sites you want to show up on and which ones you don't.

To AdSense, or not to AdSense? Tracking your conversion numbers will give you the answer you want. This invariably depends on your market. For some advertisers in some markets, AdSense is nothing but money down the drain. Huge numbers of clicks result in pitiful sales. For other advertisers, AdSense traffic is their bread and butter.

Why is it this way? Because the people who search on Google are proactively searching for solutions and are often in the frame of mind to spend money to have their problem solved. Visitors to sites like the *New York Times* or Dictionary.com, on the other hand, are more likely in search of news or quick factual information or the definition of a word, and are less likely to be in a buying frame of mind.

WHEN ADSENSE IS GOOD, AND WHEN IT'S NOT

Here are three different business scenarios. You're probably in one of them now:

- You're competing in a high-traffic, highly competitive market and you have to watch your profit margins very carefully. There's plenty of traffic available, but it's expensive. If that's you, AdSense probably will not be a good choice.
- You sell something that's high value, nichy, and specialized, such as a $35,000 software license in a particular industry. Your clicks on Google are cheap by comparison, but there are few searches on Google itself, and you only get a couple of clicks each day. Adding AdSense traffic can only help you.
- You sell refurbished XF-4431 valve controllers, and nobody else is bidding on that term. So clicks are $0.05 or less when you can get them. AdSense is probably a good choice.
- You're in a market where enthusiasts gather on discussion forums and blogs. For example, Buddhists would rarely do a Google search on "Buddhism" because they already know what it is. But the devout ones do hang out in online communities. Adsense can be very effective for reaching these communities through blogs, discussion forums, news and content sites—more effectively than Google searches.

Google shows your ads on its content network by default, so if you don't want to pay for AdSense clicks, you'll need to go in and manually turn it off. To do that, from your campaign view click on "Edit Campaign Settings." On the right-hand side you're given category options for "Networks." To turn off AdSense, uncheck the third box, and your ads will no longer show on Google's content network partners.

A HIGHER CTR STILL HELPS YOU

Getting a high CTR means you pay less money.

Remember how we told you that your position on the page is a function of your bid price times your clickthrough rate? That's a simplified explanation of Google's whole quality score formula, but it's fundamentally true. The higher your CTR, the higher up on the page Google will place you, without charging you more for each click.

That can only help your bottom line. As your CTR goes up, either you'll be able to get more traffic without having to pay a higher rate for it, or you can lower your bid prices and keep the same volume and quality of traffic but pay less. Sound like a good deal?

ANOTHER COUNTER-INTUITIVE WAY TO TWEAK YOUR NUMBERS TO SAVE MORE MONEY

More than 80 percent of your sales will come from fewer than 20 percent of your campaigns. Some keywords and ads are naturally, almost automatically, going to bring in good, consistent sales, while others simply never will. When you know which ones are which, you can put smart money and effort into those campaigns that produce and take your time and money away from the ones that don't.

It might even be 90 percent of the traffic that comes from 10 percent of the keywords. Most of the time the most productive 20 percent of keywords will be obvious to everyone, and there will be bidding wars. One way around this—and it is an extreme measure—is to turn the 80/20 principle on its head. If you can get by with a smaller amount of traffic, you can cut your costs dramatically.

An Actual Example of Knocking Your Costs Down by 95 Percent

We've been buying traffic with the keyword "Ethernet switches" and a plethora of variations. We're bidding $0.50 per click.

Let's say I go to Google and want to find out what happens if I double the bid to $1 per click. Google will give me this estimate:

| Current Clicks/Day: | 11.7 | Current CPC: | $0.33 |
| Forecast Clicks/Day: | 14.0 | Forecast CPC: | $0.50 |

Our cost-per-click will go up by 50 percent. When we crunch the numbers, what actually happens is that we'll get 20 percent more traffic but for 76 percent more money.

So what if we go in the opposite direction and drop the bid price to $0.05? Here's what Google predicts:

| Current Clicks/Day: | 11.7 | Current CPC: | $0.33 |
| Forecast Clicks/Day: | 6.4 | Forecast CPC: | $0.05 |

This shows that we will get half the traffic at $0.05 as at $0.50, but pay only *one tenth* as much for it!

Caveat: I am certain that some of these keywords will now get much lower CTRs. *We may very well lose 80 percent of the traffic, not just 50 percent.* But we'll still be paying out much less money than before. So by turning the 80/20 rule on its head, you get one fourth the traffic and you only spend one-twentieth as much money!

Reminder: You can only "invert" the 80/20 rule if you're bidding on *lots* of keywords and their variations. Use "" and [ ] keyword matching options on phrases to further specify your bids; it puts you ahead of advertisers who don't use them. As you can see, points of diminishing returns are more of a problem when you're bidding too much than too little.

With Google you can do this. Every ad is an on-screen salesman, and paves the way for real buyers to come in and spend real money with you. Some ads get high CTRs but turn away good customers. Other ads may get mediocre clickthroughs up front but end up bringing in just the right customers who buy and buy again. So you go with the ads that make the eventual sales. (The online supplement has links to more winning ads and has MP3 seminars you can load into your iPod and listen to while you exercise, drive, or work around the house: www.perrymarshall.com/supplement.)

PERFECT YOUR SALES NUMBERS AND GO ON AUTOPILOT

For almost 30 years a business called LT Sound has sold a Vocal Eliminator, a forerunner of the Karaoke machine. The Vocal Eliminator is a small unit you can play your CDs through. It eliminates the original vocals and inserts your own as you sing. Like Karaoke, but with your regular CDs. It's been running classified ads in *Popular Science*, music and entertainment magazines, audiophile periodicals, and more.

Here are two ads for this product, an early version and one that's run continuously for more than two decades:

The owner of the business, Lacy Thompson, has tested these ads for years. He knows his numbers. He knows which ads pay and which ones don't. He knows which magazines get a response, and which ones don't. He knows which sizes, which copy, which descriptions, which *everything* that pulls the best response.

The older ad above was published in *High Fidelity* magazine in October 1978. You'll notice how the mailing address is "LT Sound, Dept. HF." The newer ad ran in *Popular Science* in December 2004. Sure enough, readers of this magazine wanting the free demo are told to write to "LT Sound, Dept. PS-1." In other words, these ads are carefully traced back to the magazine they appeared in.

Lacy Thompson keeps the money flowing by knowing his numbers. And now he's got a machine that runs almost on autopilot and puts cash in his bank account month in and month out, winter and summer, year after year. The product has been redesigned a few times, but the business has not essentially changed in 30 years.

Is this a "dream" business? No, but it ain't a bad business either way. Steady. Predictable. The FTC and FDA won't be going after Lacy for anything. It's a lot better than most peoples' jobs, and there's no pink Kool-Aid® to make him frustrated with his lot in life.

If he wants to grow this business by introducing other products or exploring new distribution channels, he can certainly do that. And because his advertising is largely offline, he's more immune to competitors suddenly showing up than if he were only online.

Marketers who can do this are the marketers who know their numbers. Are you one of them? Once you learn how to do it you'll control your game.

Savvy marketers keep an eye on the numbers that matter: How much each customer is worth, what they can afford to spend to get each customer, and the return on investment for each ingredient in their marketing mix. This is true online and offline, for internet start-ups and brick-and-mortar businesses alike.

Uncle Claude Sez

Never be guided in any way by ads which are untraced. Never do anything because some uninformed advertiser considers that something right. Never be led in new paths by the blind. Apply to your advertising ordinary common sense . . . .

The only purpose of advertising is to make sales. It is profitable or unprofitable according to its actual sales. It is not for general effect. It is not to keep your name before the people . . . . Treat it as a salesman. Force it to justify itself. Compare it with other salesmen. Figure its cost and result. Accept no excuses which good salesmen do not make. Then you will not go far wrong.

Take the opinion of nobody who knows nothing about his returns.

CHAPTER 17

The Magic Number that Defines the Power of Your Web Site

The marketers who make the real bucks are the ones whose web sites have the highest visitor value, which is the average sales value of each click they get. When you grow your visitor value, it means more money getting deposited into your bank account. Plus it means more affiliates and joint venture partners will come seek you out because you can advertise more aggressively and pay more money to everyone.

■ ■ ■

ULTIMATE GUIDE TO GOOGLE ADWORDS

Every business and every industry has a basic measure of success. Retail is real estate, and the real estate in your local mall is leased on a square-footage basis, so in retail sales the measure of the store's success is sales per square foot.

On Google, traffic is charged for on the basis of dollars per visitor. So success is also measured in dollars per visitor. If 100 people come to your site and you get $200 of sales, then your *value per visitor* is $2. This is the most fundamental measure of your web site's success. Your mission in life is to have a high *visitor value*, or high value per visitor.

If you have a high visitor value, you'll be like the hottest and most fashionable spots at a high-brow mall: Nordstrom, Lord & Taylor, Starbucks, Saks Fifth Avenue, and Macy's. If you have a low visitor value, you're destined to be like the strip-mall stores: Dollar General, T.J. Maxx, Piercing Pagoda, and Wal-Mart.

If your visitor value is even lower than that, you're on the slag heap, eeking out a meager existence at a flea market, or hawking your excess inventory on eBay.

Profit is your goal. That's why you're in business in the first place. But your profit alone doesn't tell you how sleek and effective your sales process is. You might just be getting lucky with unusually cheap click prices.

Visitor value is the measure of what your clicks are actually worth. It's a measure of how smart your web site is, how effective your sales copy is, how powerful your offer is. How do you calculate visitor value? Simple:

Visitor Value = (Your Total Sales Value) / (Your Number of Clicks)

So if you make 50 percent margin on a $1,000 product and one out of every 100 visitors buys, then your visitor value is $10. In theory you can spend up to $5 per visitor to buy the traffic and still break even. If one out of every 1,000 visitors buys, then your visitor value is $1, and in theory you can spend up to $0.50 to buy the traffic.

We know this is an oversimplification of what margins are and how they work. So don't write us and complain. (Every now and then some accountant sends us a scorching e-mail about how we forgot to include depreciation or amortization or some such thing.) But the point is clear: visitor value tells you what your clicks are worth, and what you need to do about it.

174 • CHAPTER 17 / THE MAGIC NUMBER THAT DEFINES THE POWER OF YOUR WEB SITE

DOLLARS MEAN MORE THAN PERCENTAGES

Let's say you sell a book online and you've got two prices: your short version for $9 and your full, expanded version for $29. At the end of August, you make some tweaks in your sales page, and then you watch your numbers through September. Here's what you find if you just measure percentages of sales:

	Clicks	Number of Sales	Percent Conversion	Sales Amount
August	3,447	45	1.3%	$1,241
September	3,921	82	2.1%	$1,260

Hey, this is great! You had more clicks, you sold almost twice as many units, your conversion rate jumped up, and your sales dollars in September improved over August, right?

Wait a minute. This isn't an improvement at all. Your tweaked sales page actually hurt your cause. Now visitors are spending less money, and your clicks are worth less than before:

	Clicks	Number of Sales	Percent Conversion	Sales Amount	Visitor Value
August	3,447	45	1.3%	$1,241	$0.36
September	3,921	82	2.1%	$1,260	$0.32

Your conversion percentage went up, but people are just buying your cheaper version now. Now your sales process is less profitable than before, and you're less attractive to affiliates because they'll now make less money sending visitors to you.

Don't miss this: When you're split testing landing pages, opt-ins, and sales, you're not just going after high percentages. It's the *dollars* that you care about. That percentage thing is a one-dimensional view of your traffic.

Visitor value reduces a *multidimensional* process to a single number. When you try things, you learn those kinds of secrets, combining percentages with dollar values to establish how much you can bid for your clicks. Once that's settled, you move on to adjust for your own ultimate big number: your net profit.

Heck, you could *double* the value of your clicks just by offering similar products at higher price points. This is something sales percentages alone don't tell you.

Buying web traffic reduces a complex process to a simple question: *How much can you afford to pay for a visitor and still make a profit?* At first, you may not know how many visitors you need to make a sale. But you can find out pretty fast: Just buy traffic and test it.

▼ QUICK & DIRTY CHECKLIST FOR IMPROVING YOUR VISITOR VALUE

_____ An effective sales page follows the time-honored classic formula:

1. An attention-getting, benefit-driven headline

2. A statement of unique value

3. An unbeatable offer

4. A clear and specific call to action

5. An easy way to respond

_____ Continually test new headlines.

Headlines have the biggest influence on whether your visitors continue to read or not, and will make the biggest difference in your sales.

_____ Offer something clear and specific on the landing page.

Tell visitors where to go, what to do, and why it will help them. A site full of pretty images and polite puffery won't sell nearly as well as a simple, clearly-written page that tells people what they'll get if they respond today. Most of the main pages on web site www.perrymarshall.com have a specific offer and call to action.

_____ Continually change your offer to test response.

You may well find that by changing the payment terms, including a free bonus gift, offering free delivery or adding an option to gift-wrap the item, you double your sales!

_____ Add an opportunity for your visitors to opt-in.

Offer a report, coupon, discount, white paper, e-book, book, CD, software, consultation, or problem-solving tool in exchange for their name and e-mail address.

USE SPLIT-TESTING TO BOOST YOUR VISITOR VALUE

Google AdWords is revolutionary because it made split testing so unbelievably easy. Now you can test two or more ads against each other and systematically beef up your clickthrough rates over time. The process is simple, the numbers are easy to read and understand, and winners and losers are clear.

But this can also be applied to your entire sales process. You can split test two similar landing pages, two sales letters, two different e-mail series, two purchase pages, two thank-you pages—everything. *This is will multiply your sales and exponentially increase your profitability.*

Google doesn't have the guns to do this automatically with your web pages. And your webmaster may charge an arm and a leg to set up your own proprietary system for doing that. Not a problem. There's a variety of online services and downloadable programs that you can use that will run tests like these from outside your web site, but will give you all the numbers and data you need to win the game of visitor value.

One that we've been using successfully for years is Hypertracker. We put together a video tutorial at http://video.hypertracker.net that shows you how to set up this type of account to split test and track multiple sales pages, multiple opt-in pages, and more.

The best part is, if you have multiple price points for certain products, that's not a problem at all. In fact, that's the *strength* of this kind of tracking and testing. Hypertracker and other services like it can track and measure sales of different products and different dollar values. They give you the figures you need in order to discover the visitor value of your Google campaigns.

THE GREATEST ASSET YOU CAN HAVE

My first successful sales letter was for a training program called "DeviceNet Boot Camp." Engineers would come to our training class for $1,500, and we would teach them how to use a new technology. That sales letter sold a quarter million dollars of training in a year and a half.

Dang, that felt good! Knowing that every time we mailed out a couple thousand of those letters, we would get $10,000 to $20,000 in training revenue. Plus, about half the time we sent out mailers for the class, we would also get requests for custom, on-site classes.

Not only did this become a profit center for our company, it positioned us above all our competitors as experts, because we offered specialized training. All from a four-page, folded self-mailer sales letter. We got $8 of registration money for every $1 we spent sending out those letters:

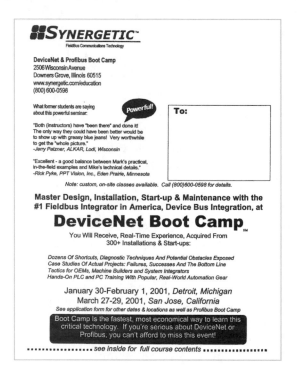

Is that a great asset or what? When you have three, four, five assets like that, especially a combination of Google campaigns, e-mail promotions, teleseminars, and direct mail pieces, you have the most liberating, profit-producing thing a business owner can have.

Uncle Claude Sez

A rapid stream ran by the writers boyhood home. The stream turned a wooden wheel and the wheel ran a mill. Under that primitive method, all but a fraction of the streams potentiality went to waste.

Then someone applied scientific methods to that stream—put in a turbine and dynamos. Now, with no more water, no more power, it runs a large manufacturing plant.

Advertisers will multiply when they see that advertising can be safe and sure. Small expenditures made on a guess will grow to big ones on a certainty.

Beat the Competition When It's Most Brutal

Your profits can grow even in the face of the toughest competition on Google. If you're slightly better in your use of keywords, slightly better in your visitor value, and slightly better in your customer follow-up, you'll move out ahead of your competitors, no matter how big they are.

■ ■ ■

Joe Spratley is a former Dilbert-cube occupant who struck out on his own. He found himself going head-to-head with his old company. It was Joe vs. the $50 million giant.

He discovered our web site and e-mailed us asking if our methods would work in his business. We assured him they would, and even gave him advice for what to do if it worked *too* well. He listened, bought the toolkit, took notes, and went to work.

We got this letter from Joe shortly afterward:

> *Last week I had an incident that made your kit worth every penny that I paid for it. My old boss, who I haven't heard from in over four years, e-mailed me to say that people at my old company are starting to get worried because I'm getting a high profile. This from a $50 million corporation!*
>
> *All I've used so far is Google AdWords and the web.*
>
> *I just had to laugh. A two-person business has a $50 million corporation worried!*

You don't have to be terrified of big players, on Google or in any advertising medium. It's a level playing field. If you follow our formula, you'll keep your toughest competitors at bay and make your biggest foes nervous. Here are the seven ingredients of a successful strategy.

STEP 1: IT STARTS WITH KILLER AD COPY

The best of the best advertisers in any market are paying solid bid prices *and* they're writing killer ad copy that would bring in high clickthrough rates regardless of their positioning. Google rewards good, relevant ad copy, you'll remember, by moving you up on the page as your CTR improves. Your bid price, however, does not change.

Below that "best of the best" are the unwashed masses of mediocre advertisers and copywriters who simply get where they are by bidding lots of money. The fact that they're there, and that even on the first page of search results are businesses with big-budget mediocrity, means that you can nudge up through their ranks simply by split testing and slowly but surely arriving at better and better ad copy.

STEP 2: THE BEST KEYWORDS ARE OFTEN NOT THE MOST COMPETITIVE OR MOST EXPENSIVE ONES

Stephen Juth's tool AdWord Acceleration tool (www.AdwordsAcceleration.com) shows you the price difference between clicks and competitors on exact-matched keywords (keywords in [ ] brackets) versus broad-matched keywords. Notice the difference in the number of bidders and the click prices for "learn Spanish":

It's usually best to bid on the three different matching options—exact-matched (in brackets), phrase-matched (in quotes), and broad-matched (without either). If you can advertise to that broad-matched lose weight traffic, for example, and make those clicks convert, you'll pay less than the huge mob of bidders who are trying to make exact-matched [lose weight] work for them.

Remember that you can filter out unwanted searches by using negative keywords. Do this and you've already got an edge on your competition.

More tips are:

- Bid on at least 200 keywords. Use third-party keyword tools like www.Wordtracker.info, www.AdWordAnalyzer.com, and Overture's Keyword Selector Tool to generate more. That's how you can get clicks at $0.05 and less.

- You may get from ten unnoticed $.05 keywords the same amount of traffic as you'd get from one competitive $.75 keyword.

- You may have a few inexpensive keywords that get lousy traffic from Google searches but a high amount of traffic from AdSense.

- You may discover that your $.05 keywords convert to sales at three to five times the rate of your $.20 or $.25 keywords.

- In any market, there are highly specific, high-priced words that everyone is bidding on and there are low-priced, *generic* words that most people can't get to work. Words like "business," "food," or "fun." You sometimes can get those generic terms to pay off if you use an opt-in and information marketing strategy to cultivate a relationship with your visitors.

STEP 3: KNOW YOUR VISITOR VALUE AND BID THE PRICE WHERE YOU'RE MOST PROFITABLE. DON'T ASSUME THAT THE TOP POSITIONS ARE THE BEST

We ran this estimate in one market. We first tried to see if we could pull anything good out of the "keyword bargain bin." We created a list of multiple combinations for the existing keywords, and then went to Wordtracker and generated a list of over 200 related words.

We told Google that we were bidding $0.10 on them and here's what we got:

Clicks/Day		Average Cost-Per-Click		Cost/Day		Average Position	
current	forecast	current	forecast	current	forecast	current	forecast
	2.3	–	$0.10	–	$0.22	–	10.8

We don't like that. It suggests only a couple of clicks per day and positioning on the second page of search results. If we changed the bid to $0.35 a click, here's what we got instead. Still not impressive:

Clicks/Day		Average Cost-Per-Click		Cost/Day		Average Position	
current	forecast	current	forecast	current	forecast	current	forecast
	5.8	–	$0.21	–	$1.20	–	8.9

At $1 a click:

Clicks/Day		Average Cost-Per-Click		Cost/Day		Average Position	
current	forecast	current	forecast	current	forecast	current	forecast
	14.0	–	$0.78	–	$10.85	–	6.8

At $2 a click:

Clicks/Day		Average Cost-Per-Click		Cost/Day		Average Position	
current	forecast	current	forecast	current	forecast	current	forecast
	22.4	–	$1.53	–	$34.09	–	3.4

Despite Google's traffic estimator often being freakishly inaccurate when it's forecasting your average position, it looked like the range for success here, i.e., getting a reasonable amount of traffic at a reasonable position on the page, would be $1 to $2 per click for many of these phrases. That's what it would cost. Are our clicks really worth that much?

Whether $2 a click is your actual visitor value or not, don't be fooled by the lure of those topmost positions—unless you've already got a serious back end sales machine that can support it. So often advertisers have been able to make positions five through ten on a page wonderfully profitable and deliver a surprisingly good amount of traffic.

But it's ultimately visitor value (VPV) that matters. Develop a higher VPV with a killer sales process, and you can bid more.

Go right now and do a Google search on "home business." This is just one of a hundred examples of keywords that draw ferocious online competition. As of this writing, the top position is going for $3.43 a click.

You could certainly pay $3 a click to be on the first page of search results, but is every click on average actually worth that much to you? If you have a fantastic sales process and your clicks are worth more than that, then staying on page one is not an issue.

But again, don't be lured by the siren song of those very top positions. In many markets, the top spots attract tire kickers and looky loos who don't turn into buyers, and those top positions come at disproportionately high prices. You need to test this. Sometimes the number-one position *is* the best position. But don't assume so.

STEP 4: SHARE CUSTOMERS AND CREATE PARTNERSHIPS

The savviest online marketers don't look at their competitors as competitors, they look at them as partners. We all know that the other guy's site is only a click away, right?

On the internet, there's no such thing as "owning" a customer or having a captive customer. Mature marketers know this so they become affiliates of their competitors and sell competitive products to their own list, and vice versa.

Approach the top bidders and invite them to become affiliates of your site. You pay them a commission for promoting you to their customers, and now you're able to multiply your visibility.

STEP 5: GET THE CUSTOMERS THAT THE BIG BOYS CAN'T GET OR DON'T WANT

Try buying exit traffic from your competitors. Buy exit pop-ups from them for example. Better still, position yourself as the alternative in related markets, bidding on the most popular keywords but offering something different. For years we've been drawing customers from Overture by bidding on that keyword and playing the role of alternative:

Overture: Beat The System
Discover the AdWords Alternative
Lower Bid Prices & Instant Results
www.PerryMarshall.com/adwords

STEP 6: MARKET OFFLINE AS WELL

If you have only one medium by which to communicate with your customers, you're always in danger of being shut off. There are times when asking for additional contact info on an opt-in page beyond just a name and e-mail address, such as telephone number, street address, fax number and so on, is the only sensible thing to do.

Bring customers offline who found you online. Run your business and stay in touch with your customers in print and via direct mail. Offer a print newsletter and create a unique continuity-based back end that your competitors don't know about.

Members of our Renaissance Club (www.PerryMarshall.com/club) receive a monthly newsletter and CD from us in the mail. It's print—you can't get it online or find it in PDF format—and that creates a second level of trust with us.

You get from us a physical newsletter in your mailbox, something you can hold in your hands and take with you to read anyplace. We don't concentrate on Google AdWords in the newsletter; instead, we deal with topics from every corner of the direct marketing and business world. It gives our customers a whole new dimension of a relationship with us, and a level of insight into doing business that extends far beyond Google.

The mailman delivers this every month, without exception. Google may not be around in five or ten or twenty years, but the postal workers will. When you're in touch with your customers through multiple media, you've added yet another layer of invincibility to your business.

You can also advertise in offline media and bring customers *online* from there, through magazines and print ads. Customers who go online from offline are of far better quality than online-only customers.

STEP 7: BUILD YOUR BACK END

The smartest businesses make their money on back end. Customers buy and buy again, and the business owner is not afraid to lose money on the initial product sale, knowing that he'll more than make it up later on in his relationship with the customer.

It's the same with clicks. If you have a killer back-end sales process, you're free to barely break even, or lose money, on the initial Google click and get that money back later. That means you can bid more.

It's harder and harder all the time to complete a one-time sale straight off a click. As the pay per click market has matured, doing that has become like riding a bicycle uphill in tenth gear.

It's almost a given in most markets, especially information markets, that your first step is simply to collect an opt-in. This gives you permission to develop a relationship with people instead of just getting a quick sale. When there are a lot of bidders, the merchants who develop ongoing relationships and accomplish more than just the first sale will be the ones who thrive.

SEA LIONS, SUNFISH, AND JULIUS CAESAR

Out in the wild, as with Google, it's not always the biggest, the strongest, or the toughest that survive, that beat out the competition. There's a saying in biology: *Runts make love, not war.*

Take the North American freshwater bluegill sunfish. The large males are always there defending their territories that the females come to in order to spawn. The smaller males, the runts of the group, behave just like females and flirt with the big males. The trick works. Along comes a real female, the courtship dance begins, the runt males join in without the big ones realizing it. The genetic material is, uh, released, and in the midst of it all, the sneaky, cross-dressing little guy contributes his share and passes on his DNA.

Julius Caesar had constant headaches of this sort to deal with. A young man named Publius Clodius once disguised himself as a woman to gain entrance into the women-only Feast of the Good Goddess. Rumor had it at the time that even Caesar's own wife Pompeia fell prey to the trick—and he divorced her for it.

Cooperative conniving is everywhere in nature. Smaller sea lions form packs and fend off the large males by sheer numbers. The smaller black-winged damselflies sneak in and get the girl while the big boys are off hunting or frolicking. Poorly-endowed peacock males form leks and together manage to win mates, despite their bigger competitors, through their collective displays.

Should you steal your competitors' business? Should you play dirty like the animals do? Absolutely not. But Barnes & Noble serves Starbucks coffee, right? The principle comes from nature: Dig for deeper niches, share your customers, pick up business that the 900-pound gorilla doesn't want, and partner with others like yourself. You'll survive. and your business will grow.

Uncle Claude Sez

Advertising is much like war, minus the venom. Or much, if you prefer, like a game of chess. We are usually out to capture others' citadels or garner others' trade.

We must have skill and knowledge. We must have training and experience, also right equipment. We must have proper ammunition, and enough. We dare not underestimate opponents. Our intelligence department is a vital factor . . . . We need alliances . . . . We also need strategy of the ablest sort, to multiply the value of our forces.

Persuasive Ad Copy: The Ultimate Silver Bullet

M any skills engage when you run an internet business: HTML and web servers and all the techie stuff; graphics, pay-per-click, search engine optimization, recruiting affiliates, setting up joint ventures, testing and tracking; analyzing web traffic, avoiding spam filters, developing products, managing projects and teams, setting up blogs, and managing discussion forums. The list never ends.

■ ■ ■

Yet there is one skill that is head and shoulders above all these things and trumps them all: copywriting. How effective your Google ads are depends on copywriting. Whether anyone buys from your web site has more to do with copywriting than anything else.

If you crank out persuasive copy, everything else will ride its coat tails. Really good copywriting is the *only* thing in the above list of skills that you cannot easily hire out. Webmasters are a dime a dozen. Pay Per Click and SEO people are not always great but readily obtainable. Products are dime a dozen.

But good copy isn't cheap. An "A list" copywriter will typically charge $5,000 to $20,000 to create a single package or sales letter. Not only that, it's no small task to "hire a voice" for your company anyway. The best voice is yours.

STRIKING OUT ON MY OWN

"I need to get good at copywriting really really fast." When I left the Dilbert Cube in 2001 and hung out my shingle, my copywriting skills were more than adequate for corporate client work: writing press releases, product descriptions, and magazine articles. However, I wanted to sell information: toolkits, books, e-books, and the like. I wanted a sales-on-autopilot business, not a consulting project business.

At the time my copywriting skills were not up to the task. I needed a mentor. For years John Carlton had been the hotshot freelancer the Los Angeles ad agencies sneaked in the back door to do the work staff writers couldn't pull off. He had just begun to mentor rookie copywriters like myself and his name was getting out. I heard he was taking new students.

I joined John's *Insider's Club* and started sending him stuff. John would rip my letters apart and bust my chops. Then he'd bandage my damaged body parts with words of encouragement and instruct me on how to reassemble my message for killer persuasion power.

Then—the first letter he made me rewrite went from 1 percent response (not quite breaking even) to 2 percent (solidly profitable). I was elated! John's guidance got me over the hump. I can attribute my business "escape velocity" to his tutelage. His help was essential to moving my rocket ship from launch pad to orbit.

(It's kind of like space travel: Your capsule either escapes the earth's gravity and circles our blue planet on its own momentum, or else it burns up in the atmosphere and sprinkles a 300-mile trail of scorched metal parts across southern Mongolia. The latter was not an option, at least for me.)

Well, then a couple years later John and I were together at a seminar and he introduced me to his number-one student, Harlan Kilstein. Harlan followed John's advice to the letter and went from zero to charging $8,000 per project in 18 months. (At the seminar, John was complaining to me about how much money Harlan was making, just by ripping off all his great ideas.)

What follows is a transcript of part of a conversation between Harlan and John. (An uncut version is available in PDF at www.perrymarshall.com/supplement.) The interview is a riot. These guys don't take themselves overly seriously, but *you* should. You should scour this chapter and adapt some of these superb examples to your own promotions. Enjoy and prosper.

> *Harlan*: Hey John, I'm holding yet another book written by an "online writing expert" who says writing for the web is entirely different than any other kind of writing. He claims web copy demands a different approach, a different voice, and a totally different attitude. "You can't write online in the same way that you write a sales letter . . ."

> *John*: He's got a lot of balls for someone who's so obviously clueless. Toss that book.

> There are circumstances online that will limit your choices of what to write, either because of limits on space (such as Google Adwords), or bans on certain words that will get you tossed off search engine searches, or get your e-mail shot down as spam.

> But these limitations are physical, such as the number of actual letters you can use in a given space. They do not mean the fundamentals of great direct response copywriting are changed. In fact, these limitations really mean that you must understand and apply those fundamentals even more diligently.

> Abandoning great salesmanship would be like firing your sales staff. You'll murder your bottom line.

> So whoever is writing that stuff about needing a different voice online is not a copywriter or a marketer—I'll bet on that.

> *Harlan*: Now, you've called me on a weak hook a bunch of times, and insisted I beef it up. How important is the hook online?

John: What makes or breaks a sales letter is the compelling hook.

It's not just important. It's the difference between copy that gets read, and copy that gets passed by.

Anyone who has followed my work knows how I have come up with some of the most outrageous and notorious hooks in modern advertising. Like—just to take the golf market—the one-legged golfer, the skinny geek who can drive the ball farther than anyone, the blind golfer, and on and on.

Outrageous? Sure.

But here's the kicker: These are all based on true stories connected with the product. (And by the way, they were never picked up by anyone else in the campaign. I had to use my best Sales Detective tactics to uncover these hooks . . . and then I had to twist some arms and put my reputation on the line — as well as risking the success of the entire project— to force the clients to run the ads once I had the hook in place.)

The Google Ad gets the first click, then the hook draws readers into the letter. It has to be so compelling and so motivating they cannot drag their eyes away from the ad. A great hook goes straight to the passionate sweet spot of the reader, and sets up camp.

A world-class hook, like a life-changing event, will linger inside a reader's head for a very long time. In a good way, of course . . . if he buys.

If he demures . . . well, he may be haunted by what he passed up.

Curiosity, desire, a challenge to your world view . . . a great hook actually violates your sense of reality on some level, or causes some inner conflict from the incongruity of what you're reading. To the degree that you are compelled to continue reading to find out what the heck this story is all about.

If you golf, I defy you to read this headline, and not care about the story behind it.

How in the world does a one-legged golfer play better golf than you? What ARE these amazing secrets?

I've taught my Insiders to think of the offline prospect as a slothful, somnambulant blob welded to the couch . . . and so averse to moving that he wouldn't get up to save himself if the house were burning down.

This may be a slight exaggeration of the actual situation . . . but not by much. Getting another human being worked up enough to take money out of his wallet and give it to you . . . is easily among the most difficult interactions you will ever face.

So the image of the half-awake blob is actually close to what you're really facing when you're trying to initiate a sale.

Your job—your ONLY job—is to get that blob so excited and agitated that he can't sleep or do anything else until he's gotten off his lazy ass and ordered your product. Because you've put an itch on him that won't go away.

The average time on a site is less than seven seconds. Top marketers keep track of these stats. Seven seconds is what it takes for a surfer to register an impression from the landing page of your site. That's not enough time to make a buying decision. It's enough time to decide, *naw, I don't want that.*

If your site were a retail store, this would be equivalent of watching people walk in the front door, take two steps in, and then turn around and leave.

That's a lost opportunity.

So, to keep that analogy, you better be darned sure that what a prospect sees first grabs his attention and draws him INTO the store.

Yet most web sites—and, downtown, many stores—actually drive people away.

Now, Malcolm Gladwell has explained in his book *Blink* exactly how people make decisions in a fraction of a second and I'm going to prove this even more so later on.

For right now, think of your hook as an actual fish hook flying out of your computer to grab your prospect and hold him in place while your ad invades his consciousness. He won't be able to click away from your site in no stinking seven seconds. His attention has been nabbed.

Take a look at this site Harlan swiped from my One-Legged-Golfer.

There's a really big promise in the pre-head and he's just getting warmed up. The headline is an exact parallel of the one-legged golfer headline hook. Only, this hook is the secret weapon of movie and TV stars and the names going up and down the side of the page prove his claim.

Your pen really does become mightier than the sword. Mightier than the best salesman you've ever met, too.

Harlan: Sometimes people ask me to look at their site and the first thing I see is there's no headline to be found. And I'm sitting there wondering why would anyone stick around and read this? Then I find out, no one is buying and it's easy to tell why.

John: The headline on the site has to tell the reader exactly what you're gonna get if you stick around and read.

Just imagine standing next to a passing crowd, say, at a football game as the joint empties. People are rushing by, eager to get to their cars or the bus or whatever, to move on with their busy, hectic lives. Their mind is still half on the game, half on the job of going home.

This is the state of your target audience much of the time—distracted, and urgently moving past you.

So, what do you say to get their attention? You can't write from your heels. You can't whisper, or be incoherent.

Rather, you need to deliver a solid punch directly to their passionate sweet spot.

> <u>*Learn these amazing moves just from watching... and be able to use them to save your life tonight!*</u>
>
> **"How A Bad-Ass Bouncer Caught The Eye Of The Nastiest Undercover Division Of The U.S. Military... Why They Chose <u>Him</u> *Over Spec Op Soldiers* To Do The Most <u>Dangerous</u> Job They Had... And How <u>You</u> Can Now Learn This Guy's Secrets To Instantly Dominating *Anybody*, Of Any Size Or Any Skill-Level, As Easily As Taking Candy From A Baby!"**

Let's go through my headline off Bob Pierce's www.trsdirect.com site. It's a study in grabbing the specific attention of a specific audience.

The pre-head promises that you can learn this just by watching . . . I'm feeding the slug factor there. He doesn't want to work at anything and I'm telling him just watch this and you'll be able to save your life tonight.

So we're hitting the most important themes: it's simple, quick, and easy to get started.

Now let's move down into the headline. We have a bad-ass bouncer which brings all kinds of imagery to mind . . . and now, oh wow, he's also part of the Nastiest Undercover Division of the Military . . . and at this point the slug is already leaning into the computer screen and that's when I reach out and grab him and yank him into my letter.

Next: You're going to be able to dominate anybody as easy as taking candy from a baby. I've got a huge claim there—the classic "Big Promise" of old school salesmanship, the key to setting up a quick sale—and to someone who's interested in the fighting/defense market, I've hit one of his most tender and influential hot buttons.

He doesn't even know what the product is yet but his insides are already saying 'I want it.'

Or check out this puppy:

> *Want to start <u>winning</u> motocross races almost <u>immediately</u>... even against stronger, more experienced, and better equipped riders?*
>
> ## Astonishing "Insider" Short-Cut Secrets to <u>Instantly Faster Times</u> & <u>Total Bike Control</u> Finally Revealed By The One Expert Many Motocross Pro's Want To *Keep Hidden!*

Notice the subtle and not-so-subtle juxtaposition of seemingly opposite concepts. If you're a motocross biker, you're going to thrill at the promise of winning almost immediately . . . even against much better riders. Hot button, punched.

And while you're still taking that lovely image in, I also promise you the insider secrets revealed by a credentialed motocross expert so powerful, other professionals don't want you to even know he exists.

Aw, the secrets promised here have got the reader sloppy with desire right out of the gate . . . and we're way under seven seconds.

If you're in this target market, you're gonna read a lot more of this ad, at the very least. Because this is exciting stuff, and it SPEAKS to your heart-of-heart and deepest wishes.

Harlan: Let's talk about bullets. Here are some of yours . . .

- How to "empty" your mind of all nonsense as you tee up—the "Zen" secret that will allow your body to *naturally "let it rip"* and instantly turn your swing into a *nuclear-powered windmill!* (You'll be the **only** guy on the course who *never* worries about his drives!)

- The tiny physics-related adjustment that will <u>*automatically*</u> "square up" your club at impact . . . *giving you the accuracy of a guided missile, every time you swing!*

- How to naturally allow that amazing "**lag**" everyone talks about (but no one knows how to tap) into your swing, *without* effort and *without* worrying about your movements! (The sudden distance you get on your drives will **SHOCK** you!)

John: All of these bullets feature what I call the "One Two Punch" tactics of piling benefit on top of benefit. You get a benefit by getting this product but there's a benefit on top of that benefit.

Most rookie writers stop at a simple recitation of a bullet. "How to get your mind in shape to hit a good tee shot." Yawn.

Go deep. Put yourself in a state where you're on the spot to drive home your point as succinctly yet specifically as a man convincing his wife to leave a burning house.

"Honey, wake up. We have to leave." Don't think so. No urgency, no sense of amazement or alarm, no insight to information that changes the way you perceive the situation.

It's more like "We have two seconds to get out of here! Flames are licking at the door already, the roof's ablaze, and if we don't leave right now we're goners . . ."

Let's look at the first bullet. If you're a golfer, when you're up at the tee, you've got all kinds of crap going through your head. So emptying your mind is going to give you an advantage, sure . . . but I'm not stopping there.

In fact, we're just warming up. Because, if you'll let us share this stuff, you'll quickly turn your swing into a nuclear powered windmill. What's more—my God, it just gets better and better!—you'll never feel anxious about your drives again. Ever.

The image is specific. The benefit is simple: Better skills than the other guys, professional-level secrets that keep you calm, and the end of nervousness over this rather difficult game.

There are two kinds of bullets—open and blind. But both employ the tease concept—one by being specific, one by being mysterious.

Here's an example of blind bullets from my infamous Total Bike Control letter:

- *Clutch control secrets for maximum traction in any kind of dirt!* (Plus—the ONE simple clutch tactic you must use to be first out of the gate! Even most pro's don't know this secret!)

- How to use your size to total advantage! (Jeff is 6'4"—usually considered a huge disadvantage in motocross. This "disadvantage" forced him to study bio-mechanics, which led him to many of his most sought-after "advantages." Doesn't matter if you're a squirt, still growing, light or heavy on the pegs . . . Jeff will quickly show you how to eliminate *all* problems and *use* your size to gain speed and agility on the track.)

- *Instantly pick your best line through any dirt with just a glance* (even if you come up on new ruts unexpectedly)! Most rookies guess, and pay dearly. Pro's know how to always hit the best lines . . . *and now you will, too!*

Notice none of these bullets gives the information the buyer is looking for. They're thinking, how the devil DO you instantly pick your best line through any dirt with just a glance? How DO you use size to your advantage? It's driving them nuts. I'm teasing them. I'm pushing their buttons.

And the *only* way he is going to get this curiosity answered is to order. I'm not going to tell him the answer until he buys the book. But he can't stop reading the bullets. It's driving him nuts.

But then, from time to time, I'll throw him a curve like these bullets:

- How to use nasty-ass ruts to your *advantage*—to gain speed, pass other riders in a blink (or force them outside), and *slash minutes off your total time!*

- How to use simple pivot and alignment tactics on the bike to keep your stamina at peak levels . . . and *finally be the MASTER of your bike!* (Easy, once you see how overlooked grip techniques and better forearm angles take the stress out of "fighting" with your bike.)

- *Instantly eliminate drift and bogging from too-wild clutch/throttle useage!* (The most common mistake rookies make . . . which murders your chances of winning! Easy fix.)

Just looking at these bullets, you can figure out what they are about, but I use powerful visual adjectives to paint a picture for the reader.

Often I will even give away the entire secret, just spell it out:

- *Braking around corners for maximum traction!* (Hint: Stay back in the seat and use your weight to come forward, over the tank, and unload as you carry your speed through each corner.) Crucial stuff for serious riders, explained in such simple terms you will understand *instantly*. (And be able to use it *tomorrow!*)

It's good, in fact, to give something away now and again. (But not when you're dealing with sex—in my Rodale Sex Letter I didn't give away any information, because it was an opportunity to go wild with the tease.)

If I were selling a book on home health tips, or gardening (which I've also done for Rodale), I'm always sure to include specific tips in detail. The sales piece becomes an information-heavy resource for the reader, who keeps it around for the advice and tips.

But the best stuff is always blind. You gotta get the product to relieve your curiosity.

This combination of open and blind bullets works like magic on readers. It teases them, cajoles them, and flirts with them until they buy.

Harlan: So why not just write blind bullets?

John: Because the open bullets serve the purpose of keeping the reader in the ballgame. Their appearance convinces him the whole thing is believable. If I only had blind bullets, their suspicions are up and they don't know whether or not to believe me.

Now there's one more ingredient I use in almost all my copy: subheads. The "official goal" of a subhead is to provide a mini-headline, typically a benefit for the next section.

Here's a subhead from an old Gary Bencivenga letter in my swipefile:

What I Learned
About the Rich and
Powerful When
I Worked at the CIA

So what Gary's done here is provide a mini-headline for the next session but it's so compelling, you just gotta read more. No one in the world can stop at the headline without wanting to know what's coming. And that is the whole goal of a subhead.

Here's another Gary Bencivenga subhead:

A Major New
Economic Trend Is
Now Solidly in Place . . .
It Will Fool 9 Out of Every
10 Investors and Affect
Everything You Own

The financial reader is looking at this and wondering . . . what *is* this new economic trend (and how come I don't know about it yet) . . . and then Gary hits below the belt forcing you into the next paragraph, ". . . and Affect Everything You Own." That's expert level force-marching readers to go further on into his copy.

Harlan: Another aspect setting your copy apart from most others are the pithy testimonials. Many people have testimonials that go on for paragraphs at a time. Your testimonials are a sentence or two and they are extremely tight.

> "John has created millions in profit for us. We pitted his ads and letters against big-city ad agencies, PR firms, and writers with lots of awards... and John slaughtered them all. He consistently hits 'home runs' for us—a 20-to-1 return in profit is not unusual. He has saved our butts on several occasions."
>
> -Robert Pierce, president, Tactical Response Solutions

John: A good testimonial is specific. "Thanks to one idea you gave me John, I made $64,212 in one week." It stretches the limits of credibility and pushes believability to the max—"I was an alcoholic in the gutter and I was just elected governor." You aim for that "Whaaaaa?" reaction.

Plus, to be effective, a testimonial has to be exciting so the reader doesn't fall asleep during the testimonials. Boring copy anywhere in your pitch will murder your results.

It doesn't get read.

Here's a good testimonial from a letter Harlan wrote. You've got a celebrity doing the selling for you. And Harlan got cute with the sub-head leading off the testimonial but it works in this case.

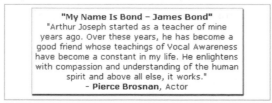

> **"My Name Is Bond – James Bond"**
> "Arthur Joseph started as a teacher of mine years ago. Over these years, he has become a good friend whose teachings of Vocal Awareness have become a constant in my life. He enlightens with compassion and understanding of the human spirit and above all else, it works."
> - **Pierce Brosnan**, Actor

Warning: *Never forge testimonials*. Good grief, especially when you're dealing with markets that are under constant scrutiny by federal "alphabet" agencies, like the FDA, FCC, SEC, etc.

If your product is any good, you can get testimonials. Just ask. Actively solicit them from satisfied customers. Most will welcome a little help in being pithy and succinct—so interview them, and help them craft their story simply and effectively.

With lots of specifics and credibility and believability.

And if your product sucks so bad you can't get any testimonials . . . find another product. Or fix the one you have. Just don't muddy the waters for everyone else by marketing crap.

Harlan: You've been doing something incredibly sneaky with your subheads for years. Here's an example out of your Rodale letter.

> ✔ A step-by-step "fingertip" guide to *the 16 most sizzling "hot spots" on her body* (pages 94-95)...
>
> Including At Least *FOUR*
> She Probably Hasn't Discovered *Herself* Yet!

You break the paragraph in mid-thought and forcibly yank the reader into the subhead. It's impossible to bail out at the end of the paragraph. Your subheads represent the second half of a blind bullet so you force someone who is scanning your copy to want more.

John: You betcha. Sneaky, and wicked-good stuff.

In the example below, I interrupt the bullet to add "and you're gonna love this"—which keeps punching at their curiosity hot buttons to the point they can not make sense of what I wrote unless they go on and read more.

But here, I sucker-punch the reader by beginning my next paragraph with the word "And." Good old-fashioned "bucket brigade" stuff.

Remember when your teacher told you never to begin a paragraph or a sentence with the word "And?" Well, forget that piece of advice. The word "and" connects you to what came before. So in the example below, not only do I pull the reader into the subhead, I drag them into the next paragraph as well.

In the example below, the subhead gives a stunning benefit. You can master these killer skills just by watching a video. No practice. No effort. It's a slug's wet dream.

And here's one of my favorite examples. This is from the famous "nickel letter" we sent out. My boys questioned why they had to mail so many nickels, because it was costing them a fortune . . . until the orders started flying in the door.

Their staff remembers the nickel letter to this day. Notice how the subhead jumps out at you. And contrary to what your English teacher told you, my next paragraph is so dramatically short that it forces you into the next subhead.

The goal of copy is to keep the reader interested, involved, and dying to find out what comes next. Move him along, as if he were sliding down a greased chute. On the ride of his life. And he doesn't get to ride unless… he comes along with you. Mint money by stringing words together, it's the most powerful skill a marketer can have.

■   ■   ■

The above content is only about a third of the conversation between Harlan and John. The full version is available in PDF at www.perrymarshall.com/supplement.

You can get a highly informative free tutorial on John's web site at www.Market ingRebel.com. And if you want to see Harlan's handiwork, visit him at www.Over night-Copy.com.

Uncle Claude Sez

People are hurried. The average person worth cultivating has too much to read. They skip three-fourths of the reading matter which they pay to get. They are not going to read your business talk unless you make it worth their while and let the headline show it.

People will not be bored in print. They may listen politely at a dinner table to boasts and personalities, life history, etc. But in print they choose their own companions, their own subjects. They want to be amused or benefited. They want economy, beauty, labor savings, good things to eat and wear. There may be products which interest them more than anything else in the magazine. But they will never know it unless the headline or picture tells them.

CHAPTER 20

Untapped AdWords Copy Ideas

I In an ad-writing rut? This will get you out of it permanently. Here's a list of ideas designed to help you think through all of the possible dimensions and directions you can take your advertising message.

■   ■   ■

Huge, huge disclaimer: Just because you see a particular type of ad in this list doesn't automatically mean we recommend that you copy its ideas. You've got to use your own critical judgment. Many (not all) of these are in fact actual Google ads by real advertisers, and some of them contain punctuation mistakes, bad grammar, stupid offers, lousy salesmanship, and more. Plus a number of them send you to web sites that sell complete junk and do a crappy job of it to boot. We're not advocating any of that. We're just giving you examples of approaches that people take.

So start your motor, turn on your creativity, and dig in.

MOVE PEOPLE BY THEIR SENSES
Words and Phrases that Evoke Taste

Designer Paint Collection
Luscious Bold Colors
Delicious Earth Tones
www.paint.com

Words and Phrases that Evoke Sound

Street Fighting Secrets
Smack! Bam! Splat!
Your Fist Against His Jaw
www.StreetFightingSecrets.com

Wordplay and Clever Language Catch the Eye

Rhyme

Be creative with this, but beware that Google's editors could decide your ideas are too far over the top, and disapprove your ads.

Stop Spam
Create a Jam
Turn Evil Men into Ham
www.SpamClam.com

Haiku

Haiku is the old Japanese poetic form that involves succinct expressions and powerful word pictures. It consists of three lines; the first and third have five syllables, and the middle line has seven.

Anger Management
Smash! Punchbowl is in Pieces
Learn Some Self-Control
www.SpringfieldCounseling.com

Metaphors
Will Your Wedding Be
A Carnival of Utter Confusion,
Or the Happiest day of your life?
TheWeddingOintment.com

GET YOUR URL NOTICED

The URL is the second thing people notice after your headline. Find out whether making it more readable or more noticeable helps your cause or hurts it; uncover all the possible ways you can display your web site location, how specific or general you should be, and which variations swing the biggest difference.

Which Domain Name Should You Use?

Choosing a more generic domain name can be useful for suggesting that you offer a wide selection of other products. Choosing a more specific domain name tells users that you're highly specialized.

15" Woofers
Extraordinary Sound Response
Top Quality Driver Design
www.SpeakerExpress.com/woofers

15" Woofers
Extraordinary Deep Bass Response
Top Quality 15" Woofer Design
www.15InchWoofers.com

Capitalizing Your URL

You can't capitalize the whole thing, but you can capitalize initials. Sometimes this makes your URL more readable, especially if it's longer or made up of multiple words.

www.adwordsstrategy.com
www.AdWordsStrategy.com
freegift.weddingsurprise.com
FreeGift.WeddingSurprise.com

PUNCTUATION

Question Marks

Google won't allow double or triple question marks (e.g., ??, ???) but you can test to see if using multiple question marks in a single ad catches users' attention better than just one.

Sexually Transmitted Info
Warts? Herpes? Blisters? AIDS?
Symptoms-Diagnosis-Treatments
www.STDmisery.com

Exclamation Point

Google will only allow you one exclamation point in your ad, and never in your headline. Test and see what effect exclamation points have.

Work From Home
Take control of your future;
We'll put you in business today!
www.epowerandprofits.com

Dashes

Don't confuse dashes, which have a space before and after ("Fresh strawberries - Low Prices"), with hyphens, which connect two words without any spaces ("Fresh-picked strawberries"). Dashes used the right way can catch the eye and even replicate spoken emphasis.

The Universe
Was it Created by God?
Or Does Science Say Something Else?

www.CosmicFingerprints.com
15,404 Clicks | 0.6% CTR

The Universe
Was it Created by—God?
Or Does Science Say Something Else?
www.CosmicFingerprints.com
21,615 Clicks | 0.9% CTR

Notice that the second ad got a 50 percent higher CTR than the first!

PROVE YOU MEAN BUSINESS WITH SPECIAL CLAIMS AND OFFERS

Trial Offer

Hoodia 750 Appetite Supp.
Rapid Loss of Weight
30 Day Guarantee, Buy 2 Get 1 Free
www.lab88.com

Results within a Certain Amount of Time

Learn German in 10 hours
After a weekend you will have a
working vocab & grammar.—Newsweek
www.unforgettablegerman.com

A Portion Goes to Charity

Diamond Engagement Rings
Free Shipping and 30 day Returns
3% donated to her favorite charity
www.IDoFoundation.org

MAKE YOUR TERMS OF BUSINESS UNEQUIVOCAL

Filter

> *Use your ad copy to filter out visitors you don't want, or to prevent clicks from people you know won't buy from you. This will lower your clickthrough rate, but your conversion rate will go up.*

Guaranteed Sales
We do the work—You get paid!
$1,995 to start your new life.
porterdirect.kokorio.com

A person who's not willing to plop down $1,995 up front won't even bother clicking on this ad.

"You Don't Have to Meet Certain Conditions"

Home Loans, Bad Credit OK
Bad Credit? Good Credit? No Credit
4 out of 5 applicants approved.
Refinance-Home-Loans.us

TAKE ADVANTAGE OF CONTROVERSY

Use the controversy that does or could surround you and your web site to attract more visitors, or more of the type of visitors you're looking for.

Sponsor a Discussion

Euthanasia
Is it morally correct?
Discuss with other youth.
NewzCrew.org

Make Bald-Faced, Controversial Statements and Claims

Global Warming: a Hoax
It's Anti-Business Liberal Paranoia
Uncover & Discover the Media Lies
www.globalwarmingbaloney.com

Have a Little Humor

How To Destroy a Village
Get the truth about the Clinton
administration. Below retail price.
www.conservativemall.org

BE A HELP IN CRISIS
Speak Directly and Solve the Problem

Bad Marriage?
Learn How To Stop Arguing, Improve
Your Relationships and Self-Esteem
www.PositiveConflicts.com

CHOOSE A TONE
Sarcastic

Spanish? Oh, Please.
Just What You've Always Wanted:
Another Dopey Spanish Program.
www.LoserSpanish.com

Hyped

Make Money NOW
Fire your Boss—Dump your JOB
You Deserve to Earn $—Your Terms!
www.businessforsuccess.net

Compassionate

Let Go Of Your Grief
Grief Is A Voice In Your Head.
Learn To Find Peace & Comfort.
www.jeffputnam.com

TRY OTHER FRESH APPROACHES

Shocking Incongruity

Tired of Sissy Men?
Meet a man with morals and
discipline of a warrior. Free!
www.worldcombatdating.com

Reverse Psychology

Do not use my program
Use other fake programs.
I love being richer than you all!
www.richjerk.com

Famous Quotes, Phrases, Lyrics

"Go Ahead, Make My Day"
Dirty Harry's Streetfighting Manual
For Hard, Leathery, Remorseless Men
www.DirtyHarryManual.com

Headline Humor

Backwards Bush Keychain
Because counting backwards makes
the time pass quicker.
www.backwardsbush.com

■　■　■

For more examples of winning ads and unusual ad copy ideas, get the online
supplement to this book at www.perrymarshall.com/supplement.

Uncle Claude Sez

There is uniqueness which belittles and arouses resentment. There is refreshing uniqueness which enhances, which we welcome and remember. Fortunate is the salesman who has it.

We try to give each advertiser a becoming style. We make him distinctive, perhaps not in appearance, but in manner and in tone. He is given an individuality best suited to the people he addresses.

CHAPTER 21

Potential Customers Are Already Looking for You on Google and Don't Know It

There are people searching online who desperately want the solution you offer. They just don't know about you yet. Use this little-known turn-the-corner Google strategy to tell them about your solution, and they'll buy from you.

■ ■ ■

Every year at Christmas time the Salvation Army sends out troops of bell ringers to stand on street corners and at entrances to grocery stores and shopping malls ringing brass bells, collecting donations, and saying "God bless you" to every kind soul who chips in.

There's no lack of Christmas advertising and soliciting already going on from relief organizations and charitable societies, from signs to TV ads to billboards to phone calls and more. So why the bell ringers? They're there to divert your attention. A ton of folks who wouldn't go looking for the Salvation Army otherwise will cheerfully give a donation if they're reminded of it on the spot.

It's the art of getting you to "turn the corner." Making you interrupt what you were doing, or looking for, or chasing after, and head down a different path. This is a vital skill if you want to reach into new, profitable markets and pluck out the big plums.

Our client Scott teaches a very contrarian approach to solving acne and other skin conditions. He argues that they are a symptom of another problem, far from being merely skin-deep. A messed-up complexion, he says, is a sign of toxins in the body. Eat a solid diet and clean up your colon, says Scott, and you've just rid yourself of a major root cause of adolescent and young adult skin problems.

Scott says he can solve your acne, but he's a nutritionist. That means if his approach works, it will solve not just acne but a whole spectrum of health problems—problems that Americans and Europeans spend millions, in some cases billions, of dollars every year to fix.

Most people who go to Google in search of a solution to acne are looking for some product they can glop on their face and get rid of the symptoms. That's not what Scott offers. Does this mean that he shouldn't try advertising to them? No, because he's got what he argues is a *real* solution to acne, and people are searching for it, so he can tell his story:

Serious Acne Alternative
Why Your Acne May Actually Have
Nothing at All to Do with Your Skin
TheAcneAlternative.net

Most people assume that acne is just a skin problem and nothing more. So the ad attacks that assumption head-on. That may be the only way to get people's attention in his market.

Again, Scott is a nutritionist, and his most likely prospect is the person who is already nutrition minded. Still, his solution to acne could double or triple his sales. Or it could account for no more than 5 to 10 percent of his total business. Either way, those are customers that he can't get any other way.

So in Scott's market, "acne" is what we call a *turn-the-corner keyword*.

HOW WE MAKE MONEY MARKETING TO PEOPLE WHO ARE LOOKING TO ADVERTISE ON YAHOO

We've got a turn-the-corner keyword or two of our own. People go online every day looking for information about Yahoo/Overture. We bid on the keyword "Overture," and our ad is there inviting people to consider the Google alternative:

> ### Overture: Beat the System
> Discover the AdWords Alternative
> Lower Bid Prices & Instant Results
> www.PerryMarshall.com/adwords

This accounts for a significant number of our sales.

We're not out to convince anyone *not* to use Yahoo/Overture. On the contrary, if you're not advertising on Overture now, you should be. It's more traffic for you.

But we're all about Google AdWords. "Overture" and "Yahoo" are *turn-the-corner keywords* for us. All the while, we can bid on these terms and make sales year in and year out because we provide the same solution they're looking for when they search on those terms: more traffic at better prices.

It's the same reason that this ad works:

> ### The Lithium Alternative
> A Rechargeable Solution to Alkaline
> Saves You Time, Money & Frustration
> LithiumAlternative.com

If you're selling lithium batteries and you know that your product is a valid alternative for certain applications that use alkaline batteries, then bang your gong and tell the world.

SELL RESULTS, NOT PROCEDURES

After all, what people who search on "alkaline" really want is long-lasting power for their electronic device. If you provide that in a different type of battery, then go on Google and tell them. If you sell acetaminophen and you know your product can relieve headaches and pain for the people who are looking for ibuprofen, then tell them.

You may already be doing this unconsciously. Now it's time to do it *consciously*. Don't limit yourself. Think of any and every problem that you offer a solution for, and then do whatever you need to do to catch the attention and sell to the people who wouldn't have thought of you but still want your solution.

Know which of your keywords are turn-the-corner keywords, and know that you need to employ a special strategy to make them work. Use seductive copy. Take a different angle, a different attitude, a different message. People *will* buy.

MORE TURN-THE-CORNER EXAMPLES

Notice the assortment of imaginative ways that these advertisers are catching people's attention and getting them to turn the corner:

Be Contrarian

Most folks who search on ADD are just trying to "deal with it"; they don't think of it as a powerful asset.

> **ADD Secret Revealed**
> Find Out How ADD Can Lead to
> Genius, Creativity & Great Success.
> www.ADD-ADHD-Success.com

You find this ad on Google when searching for "hemp." How's that for contrarian?

> **What Would Jesus Wear?**
> Fairly traded, sweatshop-free
> unique gifts & accessories.
> www.jesuswearsfairtrade.com

Be Controversial

This ad came up in a search on "evolution." It boldly plays to the modern debate.

Intelligent Design Truth?

Read why there is strong evidence
of an intelligent Creator.
ChristianityToday.com/ctmag/

The Happy Capitalist in an Otherwise Intellectual Debate

Most folks who search on "Darwin"—which is where this ad showed—aren't looking for T-shirts. But a lot of them will gladly consider the idea once you suggest it.

Charles Darwin T-Shirt

Not a fan of intelligent design?
Try some intelligent fashion!
www.therealretro.com

Warn

Flatulence: The Facts

Don't Treat Your Flatulence
Until You Have Read This Report
www.infobasset.com

Be Deliberately Ambiguous (This One's Perry's)

Organized Religion—2006

7 Great Lies Of Organized Religion
"A Hard Look at Past & Present"
CoffeehouseTheology.com

Be the Ambulance Chaser

Vioxx Injury Lawyers

Class Action Lawsuit Attorneys
Finch McCranie, LLP
www.Product-Liability-Lawyers.org

This ad came up in a search on "Vioxx."

While You're Doing That, Why Don't You Also Consider . . .

If you're searching for "Switzerland vacation," you might see an ad like this:

Traveling Switzerland?
Add Vienna to Your Swiss Itinerary
Breathtaking Scenery, Rich History
www.Austria-SwissTour.com

YOU CAN REACH THREE KINDS OF PEOPLE

This approach is how you're going to reach prospects that you might have overlooked. It's built on three possible scenarios:

1. There are people who'll gladly buy what you offer, but they don't know about you, or they aren't thinking about you at the moment.
2. You've got an alternative solution to a common need.
3. You've got a completely contrarian approach to a problem, which defies conventional wisdom.

Go after the ones who want your solution, but don't know it yet. You'll win over new customers that your competitors are overlooking. *Hit the right need and you could multiply your traffic tenfold.*

SELLING PREVENTION WHEN PEOPLE ONLY WANT A CURE

In the late 1980s, an infomercial was shot for a product that every parent should have: a video designed to help parents talk to their teenagers about drugs. Dan Kennedy, who told me this story, was hired to write the copy.

It was such an altruistic, appealing project that everyone wanted to help with it. It was hosted by First Lady Nancy Reagan; there were dozens of prominent Hollywood stars in the cast. The production values were outstanding, and it was nothing less than a beautifully produced, impressive, and inspiring infomercial aimed at making America a better place for kids.

It was the advertising equivalent of the Milk of Human Kindness. Those behind this infomercial were so proud of themselves, they almost busted their buttons. They bought the airtime and ran the infomercial. Guess how many orders they got?

Zero.

Absolutely none. The phones were silent.

Frantic, the producers called the number on the screen just to make sure there wasn't a problem with the phones. No, the problem wasn't the phones. *Nobody wanted to buy a video about talking to their kids about drugs.* And they especially didn't want to sit their teenager down on the sofa, pop in the video, show it to them, and have a discussion about it.

Nancy Reagan couldn't convince them. Hollywood couldn't convince them. A team of professional copywriters couldn't convince them.

Why not? Because the whole concept behind the video was *prevention,* not cure. It was entirely too easy for the viewer, who was in no pain whatsoever—not yet, anyway—to think, "Fred and Doris need this, not me. My kids would never take drugs. Talking to little Missy about it would be an awful conversation anyway."

It's awfully hard to sell a solution to a problem somebody's in denial about.

CHICKEN SOUP FOR THE DYSFUNCTIONAL, LUST-INFESTED DRUG ADDICT'S SOUL

On the other hand, if you run a detox center or halfway house, it's similar to owning a funeral home. Yeah, you need to be at the right place at the right time, and yes, you probably need an ad in the Yellow Pages. But getting some customers through your front door is more or less inevitable.

It's hard to sell virtue and goodness in and of itself. That's why there's such a drastic difference between nonprofit businesses and for-profit businesses. It's why there are so many novels about murder, mayhem, lust, betrayal, and hell, and so few about goodness, hope, utopia, and heaven.

Now don't get me wrong. I'm not degrading the goodness of genuine prevention. I'm just telling you that if you want to sell prevention, it's much better to sell it as part of the cure for a problem someone is having now than to try to convince a person who's never had the problem in the first place.

Copywriter John Carlton, who appears earlier in this book, has this running debate with Joe Polish, a guru of the carpet cleaning industry. Joe runs ads about carpet mites in rugs and pillows, and his ads make the phones ring.

John, on the other hand, argues that the *real* reason that Suzy Jones replies to the ads about dust mites and calls the carpet cleaner is that she's got company coming over in six hours and she doesn't want her friends to see the spot where little Jeffy puked. In other words, Suzy's going to have the carpet cleaned before the party, not after. Waiting till afterward would be prevention. Doing it before the party is cure.

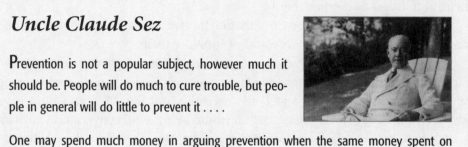

Uncle Claude Sez

Prevention is not a popular subject, however much it should be. People will do much to cure trouble, but people in general will do little to prevent it . . . .

One may spend much money in arguing prevention when the same money spent on another claim would bring many times the sales.

CHAPTER 22

How to Grind Down Your Competition: A Google Lesson from Han Solo

S ometimes the secret to success is grinding your competitors down, making incremental improvements over time until you're ahead of them.

■ ■ ■

Harrison Ford, aka "Han Solo" and "Indiana Jones," was working odd jobs back in the mid-1970s when he was asked by George Lucas to fill in doing readings for the part of Han Solo for *Star Wars*. Ford wasn't even being considered for the part. Lucas actually had his eye on Nick Nolte. Kurt Russell and Christopher Walken were prime candidates for the Han Solo role as well.

But during these test readings Lucas realized that the man perfect for the role was right under his nose. Harrison Ford was in the right place at the right time. George Lucas decided he wanted him for the part, and the rest is Star Wars history.

Did he just get lucky? Ford told *Us* magazine back in 1981,

> *Right from the beginning, I believed that staying on course was what counted. The sheer process of attrition would wear others down. Them that stuck it out was them that won. That was my belief then. It still is.*

According to Ford it was *attrition* that was the key to landing the big roles. Celebrity status and million-dollar title roles came his way because he hung in there long after other actors had given up and gone back home. Movie history vindicated his decision.

The secret to staying power, the secret to long-term sales numbers that your competitors will never beat, starts with always testing two ads against each other, two opt-in pages, two sales letters, deleting the losers and beating the winners.

SPLIT-TESTING + ATTRITION = SUCCESS

Some months back a gentleman named Brian, who had a web site that sold custom gift products for children, joined our coaching program (www.perrymarshall.com/adwords/coaching.htm). We had several productive one-on-one sessions in which we examined every element of his whole sales process and suggested changes, new approaches, and small tweaks here and there.

A few weeks into the process Brian was on the verge of giving up the ghost simply because of the amount of work involved in keeping his whole operation running, along with his perception that there were no significant changes that he could ever make that would push this site over the top into serious profitability. Perry and I managed to talk him out of quitting.

Just recently, though, we had Brian on a group call again. He raised an innocent question about conversion rates on web sites, not realizing how far out of everyone's league he had actually progressed: "I'm averaging maybe a 5 percent clicks-to-sales ratio on my whole web site. I feel like I could do a lot better and wonder if anyone else on the call struggles with this, too."

There was silence on the line.

"Uh, did you say *five percent?*" one of the callers asked.

"Yes, that's right. Why? Is that kind of low?"

More silence. Perry piped up: "Five percent is really, *really* good!"

One in every 20 of Brian's visitors was saying yes and buying from him. Just a few months before, Brian had been averaging less than 2 percent—1 in 50. What made the difference? There was no point where Perry or Bryan or Howie gave some single Eureka-moment piece of insight that allowed Brian to make the leap from two up to five of every hundred visitors buying.

No, rather it was Brian's systematic, methodical approach of split-testing our new ideas against his existing old ones and keeping the one that worked better. He did this over the course of six months and *more than doubled* the response on his web site. To Brian, this seemed totally commonplace, simply because the process had been so gradual. So unremarkable.

And it really is not rocket science. Of all the secrets that Brian and others in our Mastermind Club learn, testing is the least glamorous, and yet the single most profitable tactic. You can do this with any sales process, every piece of it, and see gradual, unmistakable improvements over time. The answer lies in *split-testing*.

GOOGLE MAKES IT *SO* EASY

What makes Google so elegant is your ability to do such painlessly easy, real-time split testing of different ads. Take an ad that's getting a CTR of 1.1 percent, write a second one with smarter copy, and run it live against the first one, and discover after a few days or weeks that you've now got a CTR of 1.4 percent. Then delete the old ad and try another copy idea to run against the new winner. That one gets you a CTR of 1.6 percent.

You repeat this process over and over again, and find that you're eventually, after several weeks or months, pushing CTRs as high as 2.5 percent or better. Maybe even close to 3 percent.

Are you patient enough to do this? Most—not all—of your competitors certainly are not. They're eventually going to tire of split-testing, if they haven't already, and conclude that what they've got going is adequate.

You can do what Brian did. He was ready to throw in the towel in March and by September had doubled his traffic, simply through his patient, methodical, little-engine-that-could mindset of never giving up while making just the slightest incremental steps forward. When you combine the power of split-testing with the force of attrition, you'll come out the winner.

NOUVEAUX SKIN CARE COMPANY GETS AN UNEXPECTED TURN IN ADVERTISING

Julie Brumlik, who sells an exotic anti-aging product using Google, happened to have a huge advantage coming into the game: Her product had already proven itself and she had been able to get celebrity endorsements, even winding up on Oprah's show.

When she joined our personal coaching program, we advised her to use her keywords in her ads, especially in the headlines. This was based on good experience; she tried it and did fine. But split-testing new ideas all the time will sometimes bring you new insights that even beat otherwise sound advice.

Julie followed her hunches and tried a different approach:

Wrinkles Instantly Vanish

Oprah, Melanie, Goldie, Demi, Nora,
Beyonce, Marisa and Dr. Weil Agree
CelebrityBeautySecret.com
2.0% CTR

As seen on Oprah

Age-Defying natural product line
for skin care. Erases wrinkles!
CelebrityBeautySecret.com
2.2% CTR

Ten percent improvement. Not bad.

Don't miss this though: Julie tried this new "As Seen on Oprah" headline, and it worked for *some* of her keywords. But not for all of them. The only way to know is to split test in each ad group and see where it works and where it doesn't.

It's no exaggeration to say that *every keyword literally represents a different market.* Julie's approach appealed to women who respect Oprah. In a number of cases it worked but not in all. Some keywords represented markets where the headline appeal to Oprah turned the trick. In other cases, it was a flop. That's the real world for you.

THE NEW ARMY OF GENERATION-X MARKETERS

A new breed of direct marketer is emerging: The one who has learned by the first-hand experience of split-testing rather than the second-hand tutelage of gurus. And he learns fast, too, because with Google and the internet, the answers are all but instantaneous. When you start to join this new and elite crowd, you'll find paybacks on a level you'd never have imagined.

This creates unexpected problems sometimes. One of our coaching students grew his business from $7,000 a month to over $100,000 a month in 12 months. A couple of months after that I got this e-mail from him:

> Hey Perry,
>
> I have been dealing with my merchant account provider for the last two days.
>
> The Bad News: They are tying up some of our funds.
>
> The Good News: We apparently "broke the bank," so to speak.
>
> We went from $103,000 in February to $175,000 and counting in March. Should end up around $190,000 or so.
>
> This is all a little scary. Hopefully I will not have any problems but, needless to say, I am applying for another account at another provider.
>
> Thanks for all the help!

I love getting e-mails from people who have problems like this! It proves that the commies haven't killed the entrepreneurial spirit in America yet.

And this guy is no old-school copywriter. I doubt he even knew what copywriting was a few years ago. He got these enormous results by steadily testing and improving his web site.

Most niche marketers don't have big enough numbers to easily test lots of stuff, and they certainly don't have a whole staff of bean counters to help them do it. So they rely heavily on gurus, "best practices," and copywriting courses and seminars.

And many of the best niche copywriters I know, people like John Carlton, Gary Halbert, and Scott Haines, haven't had tons of their stuff split-tested the way we're talking about today. Their craft is really the result of lots of experience and intuition. These guys are good enough that most of the time they can crank out a winner the first time out.

Internet marketers who split-test are mastering their trade faster than ever, and the best marketers discover what works with a combination of old-school tutelage and constant testing. The ultimate answer to every marketing question is *test it*. Answers have never been so easily within your grasp.

Now hang on, because the power of this is even greater than it appears. It's *exponential.*

THE IMPROVEMENTS DON'T JUST ADD UP, THEY MULTIPLY!

If internet marketing is some kind of magic show, I'm about to reveal to you the secret trick of the whole thing. This is what's truly important! Let's say your sales process looks like this:

1. Your AdWords ad
2. A landing page that offers a free report or white paper in exchange for name and e-mail address
3. Product sales page or sales letter
4. Your order entry page, or "action form"

We want to split-test each of these four steps. We not only test the AdWords ads, we split-test two different landing pages, two different sales letters, and two different order forms. What happens when we do this?

2 AdWords ads > 2 Opt-in Pages > 2 Sales Letters > 2 Order Forms

A challenging goal would be to double the effectiveness of each step. This is *not* impossible. And you don't have to be a genius; you just need to try some sensible things.

So if we double the CTR of the AdWords ad, and the landing page, and the sales letter, and the order form, our improvement is

$$2 \times 2 \times 2 \times 2 = 16X$$

A 16-fold improvement! Notice that the improvements multiply, cascading from beginning to end. Every improvement is magnified in the end result.

If you can triple each step, you get

$$3 \times 3 \times 3 \times 3 = 81X$$

You can make improvements early in the process faster and easier than late in the process—you have more trials. An aggressive but not unrealistic set of improvements would be:

$$6 \times 3 \times 2 \times 1.5 = 54X$$

If you go into a competitive market on Google, such as anything computer related, weight loss, martial arts, make-money-on-the-internet, real estate, web hosting, these are hyper-competitive categories that are very hard to win in.

It's not unusual to start out losing money at a 4:1 ratio, i.e., for every $4 you give Google, you only make $1 in gross profit. Not fun.

But now you double each of these four steps, and you improve your numbers by 16X. Now you're making $4 of profit for every $1 you give Google. That's pretty amazing. Continuous split-testing unlocks the whole thing like the key to a safe.

And like I said, let's take a common scenario: a sixfold improvement on AdWords, a threefold improvement in your opt-in page, a twofold improvement in your sales letter, and a mere 50 percent improvement in your order page. (Order pages are extremely sensitive to small changes. That sale hangs by a thin thread!) Now you've got as much as a 54X improvement in conversion over what you started with.

PROFITING FROM THE WINNER-TAKE-ALL PHENOMENON

The top dog has a disproportionate advantage over the others. The top three players in any market get more business than all the rest combined. This is true on Google as well, and there's a snowball effect.

You enter a market, you start split-testing right away, and you use sound marketing techniques, copywriting, and all of the tools at your disposal. How fast can you go from zero to dominating a market? Answer: As fast as you can split-test.

THE EXPANDING UNIVERSE THEORY

What you've done so far would have been very hard to do in the offline world, and two or three years ago not a whole lot easier in the online world because there was never a consistent, controllable source of traffic. Pay-per-click traffic, however, is generally consistent, and it's always 100 percent controllable. Within two to three months (as opposed to two to three years), you've tested several dozen variables and eliminated all but the best. You've polished a sales process to the point where it delivers killer results.

You're making a killer ROI on your sales process. And because you're so effective at turning visitors into dollars, you can afford to pay more for your traffic than all your competitors. You're getting unstoppable.

What now? Now we go out with our growing war chest and buy all the traffic we can get, using the Expanding Universe Theory of internet marketing.

You've started out with Google AdWords and refined your marketing machine. Now you take the same messages and sales process and roll out your product in this order:

1. Google AdWords
2. Search Engine Optimization
3. Other PPCs such as Overture and MSN
4. E-mail promotions
5. Affiliates
6. Banner ads
7. Press releases
8. Direct mail
9. Print advertising

Items two through nine are more expensive and less controllable than Google. Get it right with Google first, where you have total control, then do e-mail. Then get help from affiliates. Don't let any of these other things or people be your guinea pig. If it works on Google AdWords first, then you can invest in these other things and be fairly certain it will work. I can't overemphasize how powerful this is. Sometimes search engine traffic represents only a tiny percentage of the people who are potential customers for you.

When you roll out to items two through nine, you may make 5 to 50 times as much money as you were making with AdWords. And remember, no longer is it necessary to risk more than a few hundred dollars on a marketing campaign!

AFFILIATES: THE MOMENTUM KICKS IN

Affiliates want to make money, and the Holy Grail for an affiliate is a program that consistently sends him very good dollars in exchange for his traffic. You never want your affiliates to be blind test subjects for your experiments. *Friends come and go, but enemies accumulate!*

Do your experiments with PPC traffic first. Then verify it with e-mail promotions and inclusions in e-zines. Now that you have rock-solid numbers, take it to your affiliates.

Everybody's trying to turn their traffic into dollars. Affiliate marketing is as 2010 approaches what MLM was in the early 1990's—a craze. (It works a lot better too.)

You'll never read about this in the *Wall Street Journal*, but anywhere from 10 to 30 percent of all internet traffic is driven by affiliates. It's an invisible empire.

Affiliate marketers are not always rational, and there's a lot of ridiculous hype about affiliate marketing. But there are thousands of capable marketers trolling the web every day, looking for good affiliate programs to promote. If you're the guy with the content and the efficient sales process that spins off dollar bills, the world's your oyster.

Good affiliate relationships are extremely profitable. More affiliates breed more affiliates. The snowball effect multiplies, and you eventually hit the point where you're getting so much traffic you can't make it stop.

AMERICA'S SECOND HARVEST WINS BY ATTRITION AND WE DONATE TO HURRICANE KATRINA VICTIMS

Our business supports micro-enterprises and AIDS orphans in impoverished countries, from Haiti to Africa. Need knows no political boundaries.

One U.S. organization stands out from the crowd, however, and I originally parted with a donation based solely on its brilliant marketing approach. America's Second Harvest has an ingeniously simple message: it purchases unbought groceries from supermarkets before the products reach expiration and distributes them to the needy.

Its costs of doing this are ridiculously low, and it hits you with a clear and simple claim:

Every $1 you give provides four bags of groceries!

How could you not give to a cause like this, when you know your dollar is stretching that far?

I gave once and continued to receive mailings from them. They don't just send plain, dreary letters begging for money every time. Actually, no two mailings ever look alike. Each one comes in a different shape and size. One is a large, lumpy, clear package. Another is a postmarked lunch sack. Still another is a full-color brochure on how to volunteer with the needy in your local community.

Always full of pictures, always interesting, always fresh. At Thanksgiving in November, they wowed me with a matching promotion offer to buy 300 Thanksgiving meals for just $20. How could I not give?

Then when Hurricane Katrina devastated the Gulf Coast in late 2005, we were bombarded left and right with requests from all across the United States to donate. Even though I had prioritized giving to third-world causes, sure enough, a letter came from America's Second Harvest, saying that they were in the thick of feeding hurricane victims through their program, and would I please contribute.

It was a no-brainer. By this time the ASH letters were a welcome and regular part of every week, and I trusted them. My first gift had been small, but they kept at me. So when disaster struck and they were there again like a familiar visitor, I gave big this time.

The people behind the ASH effort are no slackers. They understand that you win by attrition. Others drop off the radar but you stand strong, and you win. You always win. This is true with Google; this is true with any marketing effort you put forth.

Harrison Ford landed the part of Han Solo through attrition and a fair share of luck. For you, it doesn't need to be luck at all. You've got Google's outstanding system for split-testing, and the flow of traffic from all over the world to vet your sales funnel.

Uncle Claude Sez

Advertising and merchandising become exact sciences. Every course is charted. The compass of accurate knowledge directs the shortest, safest, cheapest course to any destination. We learn the principles and prove them by repeated tests . . . . We compare one way with many others, backward and forward, and record the results.

When one method invariably proves best, that method becomes a fixed principle . . . . One ad compared to another, one method with another. Headlines, settings, sizes, arguments and pictures are compared . . . . So no guesswork is permitted.

. . . We test everything pertaining to advertising. We answer nearly every possible question by multitudinous traced returns. Some things we learn in this way apply only to particular lines . . . . Others apply to all lines. They become fundamentals for advertising in general. They are universally applied. No wise advertiser will ever depart from those unvarying laws.

CHAPTER 23

No More Bitslinging: Create Wealth with Your Customer List

Collect contact information and build a growing list of customers who appreciate hearing from you. By far the single most valuable asset you have as a marketer is your own well-maintained customer database.

■ ■ ■

My friend Paul Colligan would be a retired millionaire today if he had thought of this. MTV's *Spring Break Weekend 2000* was sponsored by the hosts over at www.GotAJob.com. Paul at the time owned www.GetA Job.com, only one letter different. He hit pay dirt.

Nearly naked bodies cavorting around on the screen, and MTV tells them all, "Go to www.GotAJob.com!" By the time those people get to their computer, they don't remember which is which. Paul was able to cash in on the literally *thousands of visitors per hour* who came to his site by mistake. He was making money hand over fist, all the while getting a Mach–2 lesson in online marketing.

What Paul didn't realize at the time, however, was that he was making another very, *very* expensive oversight: If he had simply collected names and e-mail addresses from those hundreds of thousands of visitors, he would have a goldmine that he could go back to for years to come.

He didn't. So the money he made—and it was terrific money—he made just once. Had he known to collect names at the time, he would be a multimillionaire today. He would have built an *asset*. (Today he does do that, and in fact teaches a method of affiliate marketing called "Affiliate Rancher" at www.AffiliateRancher .com.)

Do you want to create a growing asset that you can go back to again and again? Then collect contact information. This can make you recession-proof. It can guarantee income for you year in and year out, whether you're selling your own product or you're an affiliate of someone else.

You may be a masterful salesperson, but if all you do when people click through to your site is sell to them straight, you'll get no more than two or three out of every *100* visitors to buy. That means the other 98 leave and never come back. If they do come back, you have to pay for their click again. But create a reason for your audience members to give you their name and contact information, and you're in near-permanent touch with 10, 20, maybe even 30 percent and more of your visitors. You can speak to them again and again, and convince them over time to spend money with you. You don't have to rely on that one-time first sale.

It's so easy, too. Below is an ultra-simple page we created that captures the contact information of visitors who clicked on our Google ad and who want to learn how to do AdWords. It's at www.PerryMarshall.com/Google.

Just like this one, a good opt-in page includes:

1. The benefit-driven headline
2. A statement of what problem will be solved
3. A description, often with bullets
4. Explanation of how to get it
5. A promise not to violate trust
6. Simple information fields

Even if your site sells products that people would only buy on the first click, you can still give people an opportunity on whatever page they land on to give you their contact information in exchange for a newsletter, a series of free buying tips, a free report, or anything else of value. With those people you can stay in touch again and again.

We've been collecting opt-ins since 2002, and today we have tens of thousands of loyal readers, subscribers, and customers who we communicate with regularly. The e-mails we send out are interesting, informative, content loaded, and motivate customers to act.

We don't hit them up with constant offers, but we do make services and products available at the right time. And they respond. When you do this, you can send out a promotion and get back $10,000 in new orders in a matter of two or three hours. Your customers deliver if you do. *That is an asset!*

If your business writes software, your source code is like the family jewels. You've probably got a safe somewhere in your home or office with that code locked inside, and if you're smart, you've also got copies at a remote location.

If your product is that valuable, then imagine how valuable your customers are. It's easier to get a product than to get a customer. Your customer list takes *years* to build, and merits even more reverence, security, and protection than your product itself.

It's simply amazing how many businesses are sloppy about their single most valuable piece of intellectual property: their customer database. I don't care what you do, what you make, or how smart you are; the most valuable thing you own is your list of customers. The second most valuable thing you own is your list of *prospective* customers, those people who have expressed interest in your product or service but haven't bought just yet.

Do you capture the name, address, phone number, and e-mail of every possible person you can who visits your site? Do you stay in contact with them, letting them know what's new and always reinforcing your sales story every time you contact them?

If you know your customer list is the most valuable thing you have, then maintaining it and growing it will be your number-one priority. Just doing a good job of this will put you well above the average.

HOW YOU CAN BUILD WEALTH THE SAME WAY THROUGH AFFILIATE MARKETING

In affiliate marketing, it's no different. Even if you sign up as an affiliate and send thousands of paying customers every month to someone else and merely get a commission, you can still build an asset of your own doing this very thing.

As you buy clicks on Google, offer those people something of your very own *first,* something of genuine value that nobody else can replicate. Collect contact information from as many of those visitors as you possibly can, then send them on.

Traditionally, if you can call five or six years of history "traditionally," affiliate marketers have mostly thrown up banner ads or link exchanges, bought PPC and other traffic, and tossed it back to the original owner in the hopes that a sale will be made and he can get a few bucks off of it.

Paul Colligan calls people who do that "bitslingers." They buy traffic and get the dollars from it, but nothing else. They add nothing of value to the mix. They're just brokers of clicks, and little more. *Want to be more than just a bitslinger?* Build an asset, a customer list you can communicate with again and again.

What could you do to take a valuable product and add some value of your own to it? Here are some suggestions:

- Offer a tutorial.
- Do a substantive teleseminar on a topic that would be a natural, unassuming segue to the affiliate product or service that you're promoting.
- Set up your own site that provides a multiday e-mail course about your topic, and promote your affiliate program that way.
- Offer a free guide or reference material.
- If you're promoting multiple competing programs, offer to show people a price and quality comparison and let them choose for themselves.
- Create audio recordings on the subject.
- Hold a contest.
- Provide a free software download.

We do this with products we promote. One of them is Hypertracker. We've been using this service for years to do split-testing and to grow our own sales, and now we encourage our customers to use it and services like it as well. The technicalities of a program like that can be a little daunting. So we put together a tutorial on how to use Hypertracker at http://video.hypertracker.net. It explains the services, makes it easy to understand and use, and visitors can sign up for a free trial.

Most importantly, we don't just tell our customers, "Hey, go use Hypertracker." We don't push it like banshees. We first teach them something of value that will help them improve their own sales process.

IT'S ALL BUT IMPOSSIBLE TO DO SUCCESSFUL AFFILIATE MARKETING ON GOOGLE ANY OTHER WAY

There was a time when you could run to Google, buy clicks, and send them through your own affiliate link straight to your host's web site. Successful affiliate hosts loved this, because it meant they could very well dominate their market as almost every Google ad on the page promoted their web site.

Google saw things differently. Stranglehold setups like that ruined the whole experience of using AdWords and made Google look bad. So in early 2005, it put a stop to it. The policy now is that only one advertiser per display URL can show up on any one page of AdWords listings.

This does not mean, however, that you can't have your affiliates showing up on the same Google results page as you. It simply means that they can't just buy traffic and send it straight to your web site.

So your affiliates—or you yourself, if you're an affiliate for another host—need to come up with real, original content on the landing page, if you want to survive. When you do this, everybody wins. You add value to the market, and those visitors who sign in become an asset for you.

How to Get High Rankings in Google's Organic Search Results

P ay-per-click traffic is great, and you have 100 percent control of it. However… if you have a listing on the left side of Google instead of the right side, it'll generate at least twice as much traffic, and sometimes better traffic. Plus that traffic is free.

■ ■ ■

Search Engine Optimization (SEO) can really pay off big time. Ignore SEO at your peril! Before doing SEO, however, you need to pick your battles. Your PPC work tells you which keywords are valuable and how valuable they are; then you can selectively choose keywords to optimize for.

This chapter is by Stephen Mahaney of Planet Ocean. I read Stephen's Search Engine Newsletter every month as soon as it comes out. From the beautiful state of Hawaii, here's Stephen Mahaney with a brief but highly relevant tutorial on Search Engine Optimization.

■   ■   ■

Believe it or not, the secret to building a high-ranking web site can be boiled down to three simple steps:

1. Build a site that's easy for search engines to find and index.
2. Make proper use of the keywords that customers use when searching for your product or service.
3. Locate the so-called "important" web sites that are similar in topic to your own and get them to link to you.

Although Search Engine Optimization (SEO) can seem mysterious, especially if you're just starting out, 90 percent of it is really just focused on finding ways to achieve these three simple steps.

Of course, while these steps may be easy to understand, they can be a bit challenging to accomplish. That is why smart marketers often start out by using a pay-per-click marketing model, such as Google AdWords, to begin their campaigns. Then, once they know they have a winner, they branch out into organic search because, after all, those clicks are technically free.

In other words, if your system is working in AdWords, it's also very likely to be cost effective (i.e., profitable) in organic search as well. The catch is, of course, that scoring at, or near, the top of the organic search results can take time and patience; while a well-run AdWords campaign can drive traffic to your site almost instantaneously—albeit, for a price.

In any case, by understanding the fundamental building blocks of SEO, you'll be more able to focus your efforts on productive actions while avoiding wasted time and energy on strategies that have no effect, or worse, could even harm your page's position in the organic search results.

Remember this: SEO is not a magic art. To rank well in the organic search results, you simply must focus on building a great site, finding the words your customers are searching with, and getting the right sites to link to you.

Or, in SEO terminology, you need to build a search engine-friendly site, employ the right keywords in the right places, and get the right inbound links. Worth noting is the fact that an AdWords campaign already employs the first two of these three essential SEO components. The trick is to fold them into your organic search marketing strategy and then add the third component: link building.

HOW TO GET STARTED WITH SEO

First of all, your web pages must be easy for search engines to find and process. Unbeknownst to many site owners, their web pages are inadvertently configured to be difficult for search engines to index. And some sites are unknowingly blocking search engines from accessing them altogether—leaving their owners wondering why their site isn't doing better in the search results.

Whether it's long and uncrawlable dynamic URLs, poor use of page redirection, pages using images when they should be using text, or over-reliance on Flash and JavaScript, there's no end to the ways to kill a site's ability to be indexed by search engines. Although the technical details for dealing with each of these maladies could fill a book, you'll be pleased to know that Google offers a service called "Google Sitemaps" that's designed to make sure your pages get into Google, no matter how search engine unfriendly those pages might be (within reason, of course). You can find it at:

www.google.com/webmasters/sitemaps

For a more indepth analysis of how to fix the technical glitches that scare off search engines, check out a good SEO manual like the Planet Ocean's *Unfair Advantage* book (www.PlanetOceanNewsletter.com).

However, making your site search engine-friendly by itself won't propel you to the top of the rankings. A search engine-friendly site is actually more about avoiding the mistakes that will damage your search engine ranking than it is about reaching the top of the search results. To achieve that top rank, it's important that you take the next step and understand the interrelated role that keywords and inbound links play. To put it simply:

Keywords tell search engines what your page is about.

Inbound Links tell search engines that your page is important.

As you can see, because links identify your site as important, they are the key factor in determining exactly where your pages will rank in the search engines.

Although keywords are a critical part of search engine optimization, their direct effect on ranking is obscured by the fact that inbound links—and the keywords found within those links—actually have a far greater effect on ranking than the keywords found on the actual web page. In fact, we've even seen cases where high-ranking pages don't even contain the keyword that they are ranking for. In every such case, the page has inbound links that contain the keyword in the visible text of the link (also known as the anchor text).

Still, similar to AdWords, finding the right keywords does play a crucial role in letting a search engine know what search queries your pages should be displayed for, and you should be sure to place your best keywords into your web page's viewable content.

However, from a strict ranking perspective, you'll find that building quality incoming links to your site is the most effective approach you can take when it comes to ranking well over the long run. In fact,

> *a link to your page from an important site that uses your keywords in the anchor (or viewable) text of the link will likely produce a more positive ranking effect than all of your other ranking efforts combined!*

That's why link building is such an important component of getting your web pages ranked highly in the search engines.

BE REALISTIC IN YOUR TIME-FRAME EXPECTATIONS

Getting to the top of the search engine results for popular keywords is a gradual process. Chances are some of your competitors may already have a fairly robust SEO program up and running. It's possible they've been on the web for a long time, and these days, time is a search engine optimizer's greatest friend, or worst enemy— depending on your perspective. If a search engine has already determined that your competitor is the most relevant site for a particular keyword, then you should expect that it will take some time and effort to make that search engine change its mind.

Achieving top listings for a top keyword can often take six months to a year. The typical scenario is that you'll continue to gradually gather more and more relevant links while you improve the overall quality of your site. Then, all of a sudden, boom—you're at the top of the search results. For competitive keywords, that's the only way it can be done (a fact that can make life difficult for professional SEOs because so many clients unrealistically expect immediate results).

Again, that's why so many professional online marketing specialists use pay-per-click (AdWords) to gain the immediate traffic they need to test their systems and juice their profits. This buys you time while your organic search strategies are allowed to grow, mature, and ultimately blossom into top rankings.

In the long run, top results in organic search can become a cost-effective money-making machine, provided your strategies are patiently built on a solid strategic foundation focused on building valuable content and getting links from important, topically related sites.

KEYWORD SELECTION FOR ORGANIC SEARCH RANKING SUCCESS

If you have experience in keyword selection for an AdWords campaign, you'll find there are many similarities that transfer nicely to search engine optimization. For example, an AdWords campaign might focus on finding overlooked and underutilized keywords in order to get clicks for cheap.

In SEO, pages can be built around the concept that these overlooked keywords will also be easier to rank for in the organic search results, especially in the beginning stages of optimization. Wordtracker is a great tool to find these bargain keywords, just as in pay-per-click keyword selections.

Planet Ocean's *UnFair Advantage Book on Winning the Search Engine Wars* devotes an entire section to keyword selection strategies. There you can learn how to find the right keywords that allow you to get easy customer traffic from niches that your competition has overlooked.

Just be sure to bear in mind that if you're competing only in popular keyword searches where the majority of your competition is focusing their efforts, you'll need lots of really good links to get to the top of the organic search results. By no means is that impossible—it just takes time.

KEYWORD PLACEMENT FOR ORGANIC SEARCH RANKING SUCCESS

To succeed in the organic search results over the long term, it's important to get your best keywords inserted into the appropriate places. Clearly there are on-page keyword placement locations, but there are also off-page locations that are even more effective, ranking-wise.

On-page locations include:

- Title tag
- Meta Description Tag
- Headline tags
- Body copy

These are the most critical placements. In addition there is "proximity" to consider. This is especially true when optimizing for two or more combined keywords that make up a keyphrase. It's better to place the keywords that make up a keyphrase close to each other. Also, it's better when the keywords appear early in the page's content. Usually, the earlier the better.

Off-page locations include:

- The anchor text of your incoming links
- The URL itself

Having your keywords or phrase in the actual link that points to your page is very, very important. And having the keyword or keyphrase in the URL itself tells both the search engine and the potential site visitor that the page is relevant to the keyword being searched.

HOW TO GET NATURAL LOOKING LINKS FROM IMPORTANT PAGES

One of the trickiest aspects of SEO is the process of building high-quality incoming links. It's also the single most important thing you can do to improve your rankings.

The challenge for most sites is to accumulate enough incoming links to appear relevant to the engines *without* tripping any one of the many spam filters and penalties that are applied to sites that cheat. The secret to getting it right is to take the search engine's point of view (SEPOV) when building your incoming link structure.

The key point to remember is that search engines like natural link structure. They hate artificial link structure. Some of the qualities associated with an "artificial" link structure are:

- Inbound anchor text is identical.
- Inbound link count increases suddenly.
- The site links out to link farms or web rings.
- A high percentage of links are reciprocal.

Here are some of the qualities associated with a "natural" link structure:

- Inbound anchor text varies.
- Inbound link-count increases gradually.
- The site links out to only reputable pages.
- Links are rarely reciprocal.

From search engine's point of view (SEPOV), natural links vary in anchor text, whereas artificial links tend to be identical. Natural links increase gradually over time as referral sites add links one by one. Artificial links can sprout in great numbers all of a sudden. When they do, the search engine often suspects they are either purchased or artificially manipulated in some other way.

Sites designed around natural links don't usually swap links, so their outgoing links tend to point to pages that are already known by the engine to be in good standing. Oftentimes these pages have been indexed for many years and may even be whitelisted—a term that identifies trusted sites that are somewhat impervious to penalty.

Artificial links, however, often rely heavily on link exchange tactics, in which the sole purpose of the link is reciprocity—having little or nothing to do with adding value for the site visitor by way of linking to worthwhile content. Sites designed around artificial links will have outgoing links that point to pages that resemble link farms, web rings, or isolated nodes (i.e., groups of pages linking to each other but lacking inbound links from outside trusted sites).

Keeping these facts in mind, one should strive to build the most natural-looking incoming-link structure possible. From SEPOV, the best kinds of links are unrequested links. The engines are looking to bestow high rankings on only those pages that people voluntarily link to due to great content—not because some webmaster has spent a lot of time swapping links.

CHOOSE YOUR LINKS WISELY

The best kinds of links are from authoritative pages. Such pages are considered important and are usually identified as such by Google using its PageRank scoring system. A simple rule of thumb is this: The higher the PageRank, the better the link. Directory examples would include sites like Yahoo and DMOZ. Others sites like PBS.org, National Geographic, CNN, or ZDNet would be exceptional authoritative links regardless of topic.

GET LINKS FROM TRUSTED PAGES THAT MATCH YOUR TOPIC

Your next best option is to acquire links from pages that are trusted. Trusted pages are sites that have been indexed for a while and have already been assigned a Google PageRank—usually PageRank 5 or better.

It helps even more if these pages are on-topic—i.e., they match the topic of your page. Links from on-topic trusted pages can give you a significant boost in rankings.

COUNT THE NUMBER OF LINKS ON THE REFERRING PAGE

Another point to remember is the fewer the number of links on the referring page, the better. Ideally, the referring page would have only one link, and it would be to your page. Of course, that's rarely practical. But having your link on a page with 100 other links is much less effective because the value of your link will be divided by the number of links on the page, a condition we call *link dilution*.

While easier said than done, the ideal would be to get your incoming links from popular, on-topic, high PageRank pages that have few outgoing links and are found on trusted sites. And if you can control how those links appear (in terms of your keywords appearing in the anchor text), you'll be in even better shape.

AVOID GETTING INVOLVED WITH RUN-OF-THE-SITE LINKS

Avoid run-of-the-site links. These are links where every page of a site links to your homepage. When you have, say, 1,000 incoming links all originating from subpages within the same site, it appears to Google that your link count is artificially inflated.

MAINTAIN CONSISTENCY IN THE FORMAT OF YOUR INCOMING LINK URLS

You may not be aware of the fact that the following pages are technically four different URLs from the SEPOV, in spite of the fact that each of them will land the site visitor on the same page.

1. http://your-site.com
2. http://your-site.com/index.html
3. www.your-site.com
4. www.your-site.com/index.html

If those who link to you use four different URL formats to point visitors to your home page, then your page's popularity is being diluted by a factor of four. This is not good!

Therefore, you should do everything in your power to standardize your incoming link URL-format in order to consolidate your page's popularity (i.e., PageRank). Doing so will produce the maximum relevancy boost possible from your incoming links.

GET YOUR KEYWORDS INTO YOUR ANCHOR TEXT

It's very important that you get your keywords into the text of the link (anchor text) that other sites are using to point visitors your way. True, this may be difficult with directories unless the name of your company includes your keywords. Regardless, the boost in keyword relevancy is significant enough that it's worthwhile to contact everyone who is linking to you with a specific request regarding the text being used in your link.

If you happen to be selling model airplanes, then anchor text such as "airplane models" or "model airplanes" will be infinitely more valuable to your relevance efforts than anchor text simply saying "click here." From the SEPOV, the former states the topic of your page while the latter gives the engine no clue whatsoever what your page is about.

A word of caution: it will look more natural from the SEPOV if the text links that are pointing to your site are not all identical. Strive to maintain slight variations, as would occur if the sites that are maintaining those links were generating the anchor text independent of your influence.

Of course, the nature of your business and the name of your company might dictate the range of options available to you. However, do everything in your power to ensure that the text being used to point visitors and engines to your site looks natural from the SEPOV. This strategy can make a *huge* difference. Generally speaking, from the SEPOV, the anchor text is one of the largest influences in determining the topic of your web page.

Go for Deep Links

Make sure that some of your links are deep links – i.e., links to sub-pages within your site other than your homepage.

Beware of the "Nofollow" Tag

See to it that your incoming links from off-site pages do not include the rel="nofollow" attribute within the source code of the link. Nofollow renders the link useless to your ranking efforts because Google doesn't credit your page for having that incoming link.

BE CAREFUL WHO YOU LINK TO!

Avoid anything that stinks of an artificial effort to manipulate the engines. Linking to these sorts of unnatural linking structures can get you penalized, so always be very careful about who you link to.

Here are four cautionary steps you should take before linking to other sites:

1. Search for their domain name on Google and Yahoo. If they're not listed on one or either of the engines, that's a bad sign. Linking to them could get your site penalized and possibly banned. However, if they are listed, you can proceed to step two.
2. Determine who is already linking to them. The more incoming links they have, the better. And the more important the sites that are linking to them, the better. Their PageRank score is one indicator of how important Google thinks the site is.

    Beware of linking to sites or pages with a PageRank=0. This could mean that Google has penalized them. Granted, this test may not apply to very new sites, but if a site has been around for a while and lacks any PageRank, then you should be wary of linking to it.
3. Avoid linking to sites with controversial topics. Good examples of such sites would include gambling, adult, pharmacy, or loan/debt sites (unless you happen to be in one of these industries and the topic matches the content of your page).

Remember: You can definitely be hurt by who you link to, so choose your link partners carefully.

TRAIN YOUR EYE ON THE PRIMARY GOAL—PROFITS!

Of course, our biggest assumption is that you're optimizing your site with profits in mind. That being the case, you'll want to always focus your efforts on strategies and relationships that will generate the most revenue relative to effort. Therefore, look first for link relationships that will produce traffic that fits the profile of your customer market.

While it's true that incoming links from just about any site provide a slight boost to your page popularity (leading to better search engine ranking), such links all too often fail to produce targeted traffic, which is what you really should be looking for. This is one of the many reasons a link from a topic-related site is immeasurably better than a link from an off-topic site.

THE BEST PLACE TO START GETTING LINKS

Rather than swapping links (which should always be your very last strategy), consider some of your alternative options for acquiring incoming links. Probably the best place to start is by submitting your site to web directories. Besides the two mainstays—Yahoo Directory and DMOZ—there are others that come and go with the winds of change. Refer to Planet Ocean's "Ultimate Directory List" at:

www.searchenginenews.com/se-news/directory-master.html

There you can see which ones are currently worth your time and effort to submit to.

Some of these directories are free and some charge a fee that when considering the value of your time, might be worth it to get a new site's foot in the link-popularity door. To add your site, look around on the directory's main page for a link that says something like "Add URL," "Suggest URL," "Add Your Site," or "Suggest a Site." Follow that link to get details about exactly how to add your site to their directory.

By the way, to avoid unnecessary delays in getting listed, be sure to submit your site to the proper category within each directory. Submitting your site to the wrong category can result in a ridiculously long delay or simply not getting listed at all. Remember that the directory editors receive an enormous number of site submissions, so save yourself some grief by carefully considering exactly which category your site belongs in before submitting.

Also, when getting listed in directories, be sure they provide a direct, static link to your site. Some directories will send your link to a computer program running on their own servers so they can track who clicked on the link and then send the link on to your site. This is called a redirected link, and is useless for boosting search rank. It is not a concern with most major directories, as they tend to use direct links. However, many smaller directories like to redirect their links. Although this may add to your traffic count, it does nothing to help your search engine ranking efforts. That's because engines fail to see the connection between the redirected link and your site's actual URL.

LINK OUTSIDE THE BOX

Figuring out where to get your incoming links from is like solving a puzzle. It takes a little creativity coupled with following various formulas and patterns. Ask yourself, who else has a site that might benefit from linking to me?

Suppliers you do business with or professional organizations you're involved in might be willing to list you on their referrals page. Legal advisors, accountants, or financiers you do business with might also like to list you as a client or maybe showcase your business in their online portfolio. Your employees may have blogs or personal home pages that could link to you, and so forth.

Here are a few more ideas to help spark your creative link building efforts. Many online business owners write articles about topics related to their sites. Then they offer to let other sites use them as content in exchange for a link back to the author's site. You're probably an expert in the business you're in and therefore an authority on certain subjects that may lend themselves to interesting reading.

"Swap" links with a partner company that you closely do business with—or whose services complement your own. Look for business partnerships with other web sites that are useful to your own customers and whose customers are useful to you.

Look for compatible (but not competing) businesses, and then form a partnership where you link to each other actively through mutual promotion. Not only can this bring in new traffic and boost your PageRank, but you may also develop important business relationships this way.

THE POWER OF PRESS RELEASES FOR SEO

Press releases are an excellent way to gain relevant links to your company's site. Again, be creative. Chances are that there are a number of reasons (product launches, staff additions, promotions, partnerships, new services, etc.) you can find to release news about your company to the press. The engines quickly pick up press releases and the links contained within them are typically trusted. They also tend to remain on the web for a good long time.

Another interesting way to promote your own site is to submit testimonials, along with a link to your site, about products you are really enthusiastic about. If the testimonial is well written, the company will often post it on its site.

Here's one of the most potentially productive tips: Find out who's linking to your competitors and convince them to link to you instead. Go to Yahoo and enter the following in the Yahoo search box:

linkdomain:www.your-competitor.com-site:www.your-competitor.com

You'll learn who you should contact. (Replace your-competitor.com with one of your competitor's domain names.)

Bear in mind that whenever you're successful in getting someone to switch their link to you, you gain twice: once for gaining a new link and a second time for reducing the incoming link count of your competitor.

If the link is an especially good one (an authoritative site in good standing with great incoming links, few outbound links, and high PageRank), then pay it if you have to. Offer it a better deal than the one they have (if any). Do whatever it takes to get those quality links! Write it off under the cost of advertising.

By using your imagination and dovetailing the nuances of your own business into the mix, you'll no doubt discover a plethora of opportunities for gaining legitimate incoming links.

THE PROBLEM WITH RECIPROCAL LINKS

When all else fails, you may begin considering reciprocal links. We don't like this strategy all that much because search engines are continuously getting more sophisticated about detecting artificial linking patterns. Unfortunately, one of the most artificial linking patterns is reciprocal links, because natural link patterns are not typically reciprocal.

If Yahoo lists a site in its directory, that site doesn't routinely link back to Yahoo. Of course, there are plenty of exceptions, but the engines are still looking for pages that rank well due to popularity based on content. They want to avoid sites where it appears the webmaster has spent a lot of time swapping links. In fact, it's entirely possible the two swapped links are discounting each other based on an assumed link exchange arrangement that looks contrived from a search engine's point of view.

EVALUATING THE QUALITY OF A LINK

Modern link building strategy is all about topical relevance. In other words, pages that link to each other should cover similar subjects. The closer the two pages are in topic, the better the link is likely to be perceived by the search engines. This rule applies both to the sites that are linking to you and to the sites you're linking to.

As ranking algorithms become increasingly advanced, search engines are evaluating web sites in terms of neighborhoods of related sites. By linking to, or being linked from, an unrelated site, you're venturing out of your neighborhood. Sometimes search engines view this suspiciously.

The most valuable links are from web pages that feature content related to your site. Links to or from off-topic pages are less useful, and in some cases, too many of these off-topic links can even be harmful to your site's search engine rank.

As search engines evolve and become harder to manipulate, links from important sites within your niche will continue to grow in value. This is the key to establishing your site as an important destination from a search engine point of view.

DON'T SWEAT THE SMALL STUFF

Of course, you can't always control who links to you, so there will be exceptions to the neighborhood rule. This is actually not a big deal. Every site has a few off-topic links pointing to it. In fact, a small amount of off-topic links makes your linking structure appear even more natural. But you should strive to make the bulk of your incoming links come from topically relevant sources.

WHAT REALLY SMART ONLINE MARKETERS DO . . .

Smart online marketing professionals are multidimensional in their strategies. They seldom put all of their eggs in a single basket. This is especially true in regards to pay-per-click and organic search marketing efforts. Because so many aspects of the two strategies run parallel to each other, it makes good sense to understand how both work and employ them together so your efforts are working double-duty.

As you test your keywords, benefits, and features to learn what's working in your AdWords campaigns, it just makes sense to redeploy your successes along the parallel path of organic search as well. Failing to do so means you are probably leaving easy money on the table! Sometimes a LOT of money! We know of instances where successful AdWords campaigns have laid the groundwork for enormously successful and very long running organic search marketing campaigns—and at a fraction of the overall cost of maintaining the initial pay-per-click endeavor.

As mentioned, success in the organic results takes some time and patience. AdWords is quicker but arguably more expensive. However, by using AdWords to help you test and map out your organic strategies, it's possible to build a long-term cash cow with the potential for success that can run indefinitely and at a cost so low it's borderline absurd.

Bear in mind that this chapter is merely an organic SEO strategy primer. Therefore, I will close by highly recommending the following three resources because this is where we've obtained all of the info within this chapter, reprinted with permission, of course, as a sampling of Planet Ocean's indepth research and useful resources:

1. *Planet Ocean's Beginner's Guide to SEO*, http://Guide.PlanetOceanNewsletter.com
2. *The UnFair Advantage Book on Winning the Search Engine Wars*, http://Advantage.PlanetOceanNewsletter.com.
3. *Planet Ocean's Members-Only Monthly Publication*, SearchEngineNews.com, www.PlanetOceanNewsletter.com.

Planet Ocean has been specializing in teaching people how to rank their sites at the top of the organic search results since 1997. It is a pioneer in the field and remains one of the foremost authorities on the subject, a trusted source for solid, long-term SEO strategy. It is the resource we use when mapping out our own organic search marketing strategies.

CHAPTER 25

Google's Tools for Smarter AdWords Results

The process in this section gives you that last 1 percent of knowledge that makes you sharper than your competitors and smarter about your own market. That means you'll have better ability to grow faster by attracting more customers, and more long-term staying power in your business.

■ ■ ■

In 1996, the Chicago Bulls won its fourth NBA title, and Michael Jordan, the star of the team, grossed $80 million. Jordan's teammate Joe Kleine made $272,250 that year. Heard of Joe? Probably not.

Jordan takes the Bulls to the world championship and earns 294 times as much money as his teammate. Does that mean, therefore, that Michael Jordan is 294 times as good a basketball player as Joe Kleine? Not at all.

So why the difference in pay? Simply put, Michael Jordan drives sales of basketballs, tennis shoes, T-shirts, soft drinks, and toothpaste in Paris, Barcelona, Buenos Aires, Tokyo, Melbourne, Johannesburg, and Davenport, Iowa. Joe Kleine doesn't.

In the words of Thomas Friedman, author of *The Lexus and the Olive Tree* (Anchor, 2000):

> *The gap between first place and second place grows larger, and the gap between first place and last place becomes staggering. In many fields there is rarely one winner, but those near the top get a disproportionate share.*

How would you like to be the winner who takes all? How would you like to have that disproportionate share?

KNOW WHO YOUR VISITORS ARE: GOOGLE ANALYTICS

The conversion tracking that's built into Google AdWords gives you a skeletal view of how well your keywords are producing individual actions like opt-ins and sales. Google Analytics goes deeper to connect those keywords to very specific visitor activity everywhere on your site.

Google now gives you graphics and reports that tell you that much more about who is finding you on the internet—and when, and where, and how, and how long. With Analytics you can know:

- How many visits your site gets, daily and hourly
- What web sites your customers are coming from
- Where your visitors are finding you around the world
- How much time visitors spend on each of your pages
- Where your potential customers are bailing out
- What order they click from page to page
- What browsers, platforms, screen sizes, and connection speeds your visitors are using
- And much more

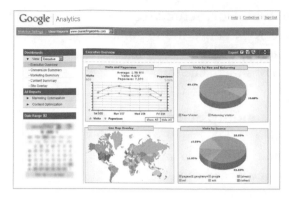

This really is a great tool, but there is one caveat. Because you're paying Google all this money for clicks, it's questionable to rely on it to also tell you what those clicks are bringing you. You might consider other tools like www.VisitorVille.com, www.Hitslink.com, and www.ClickTracks.com.

TRACK YOUR MOST PROFITABLE ADS AND KEYWORDS: GOOGLE REPORTS

Do you want to know not only just how many opt-ins you're getting but also sales, too? Do you want to know which of your ads is selling more? That's information you simply cannot get from your regular campaign summary in Google AdWords. But you can get this from Google's reports:

- Your URLs' clickthroughs and conversion rates
- Leads, opt-ins, sales, and sign-ups for all of your campaigns
- Conversion percentages, not just CTRs, for each of your ads
- The selling power of your image ads
- Sales and conversion numbers for your targeted sites
- Much more

You'll sometimes make the surprise discovery that between two ads you've been running, the one with the higher CTR is *not* the one that's resulting in more signups or sales. For example, suppose that these two ads are competing for a higher CTR:

Astronomy, Science & God

Where Did the Universe Come From?
Latest Info from Hubble Telescope
CelestialMechanic.com
834 Clicks I 0.4% CTR

Astronomy, Science & God

Where Did the Universe Come From?
Latest Info from Hubble Telescope
CosmicFingerprints.com
626 Clicks I 0.3% CTR

You'll take the first one hands down, right?

But wait: run a report on the conversion rate and you may discover that the visitors from the second ad are converting at 25 percent (for a total of 157 sign-ups) while the first ad is converting only at 15 percent (for a total of 125). Guess which ad you're going to stick with?

This second level of knowledge gives you a whole new edge in the market. Now you're not merely earning more clicks; you're creating more profitable, better converting advertisements.

BID SMARTER: EDITING CPCS AND URLS FOR INDIVIDUAL KEYWORDS

You don't have to stick to one single bid price for every keyword in your ad group across the board. Nor do you have to send all of the traffic for every keyword to the same destination URL. To edit this, select the keywords you want to tweak and click on the "Edit Keyword Settings" button just under the ad:

You can tell Google where exactly to send the traffic for each of the keywords in your list. You can edit CPCs as well. And you can direct each keyword individually or click on the orange "V" button to set the same value for the whole list. Here's what it looks like for a set of our keywords:

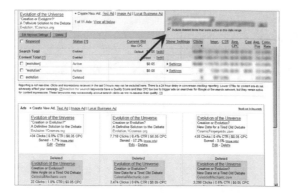

TRACK YOUR PROGRESS: CHECKING BACK OVER YOUR OLD DELETED STUFF

Did you delete a keyword unintentionally? Are you trying to remember the exact wording in that old ad you wrote but have since deleted? In each ad group, you can look back at deleted items. This ad group even has an old keyword leftover from the days when Google used to disable them. And you can look over old deleted ads as well:

A word of caution, though—don't panic if it looks like old deleted items had a better CTR than your current ones. There's one of two perfectly reasons why the deleted ads in the example above show higher CTRs than the current ones:

1. I've since turned on content-targeted traffic, which earns lower CTRs.
2. The market was different back when I was running the deleted ad, and the ad I have running now was actually doing much better than 0.8 percent at the time.

TWEAK YOUR CAMPAIGN SETTINGS

You can choose certain parameters and settings for each of your different campaigns, and all of the ad groups in that campaign will follow suit. You can:

1. Rename your campaign
2. Adjust your daily budget
3. Plan for your ads to stop showing after a certain date
4. Adjust your ad rotation
5. Turn search network ads on or off
6. Turn content network ads on or off
7. Bid separate prices for content network ads
8. Change your target languages
9. Change your target geographic locations

To make these changes, click on the "Edit Campaign Settings" link near the top of your page:

WHAT ABOUT AD ROTATION?

If you're split-testing two or more ads in an ad group, Google will automatically show the better-performing one a higher percentage of the time, unless you tell it otherwise. In your campaign settings, the box next to "Show better ads more often" is automatically checked. You can turn this off.

These two ads below have that feature disabled, and they're showing fairly evenly. Google tells you right under the CTR how much each ad is "served." It will never be exactly 50/50, and it can sometimes vary as unevenly as 60/40.

Disabling this makes your split tests go faster. So I always do, if I'm watching a campaign closely. If not, I leave it enabled. This is kind of like the difference between an automatic transmission and a stick shift. You get to choose.

SHOULD YOU USE GOOGLE'S BUDGET OPTIMIZER?

This is an option in your campaign settings. It's listed under "Advanced Options" in the category of "Bidding."

Let's talk about this. With this feature, you tell Google what your daily budget is, and it'll set your cost-per-click for you automatically to ensure that you get the maximum number of clicks each day without going over your spending limit.

Here's what Google says about it:

> You won't be able to edit or view your original Max CPCs in your Ad Groups. The Budget Optimizer will set new keyword max CPCs and adjust them for you.

So should you enable this, or not? The *real* question here is this: Do you want Google to be setting your cost-per-click for you? Google has no way of knowing what your VPV is. It'll set your CPC to a certain amount based on how many possible clicks they believe they can get out of you. The actual profitability of your sales process and your strategic position on each search page means nothing to

Google, which means it's very likely to spend more of your money than your clicks are actually worth.

Our answer: *You* be the one deciding your CPC, not Google. Your decision on how much to spend on your clicks is all based around your VPV, or your visitor value—the average amount of money each visitor spends with you. Only you know that. Google doesn't.

WHY THE IDEA OF A MARKETING BUDGET IS DEEPLY FLAWED

Unfortunately, for most companies who don't track the actual dollars-in-dollars-out profitability of their marketing, their advertising expenditures have to get stuck under the same constraints as the rest of their spending. But now think about this: If you know that you're getting back $1.50 for every $1 you spend in marketing, then why would you ever put a budget limit on it?

You see, the idea of a marketing budget is fundamentally flawed. Marketing is an investment, once you've gotten it into profitability. The only limit to it is that each single venue you advertise in, e.g., an ad in a particular magazine, is only so profitable, and you don't want to spend more money on that one venue than it can possibly hope give you back in profits. Advertising does reach a point of diminishing returns.

But it's much more about finding a "sweet spot" than trying to operate under a budget. With a single marketing medium like Google, you just test and find out which cost-per-click results in the biggest bottom line for you, and then you leave it there. Don't let Google do this for you. That would be like the fox guarding the henhouse, or leaving the German shepherd to look after the pot roast!

WHEN YOU NEED TO SET A SPENDING LIMIT

If you're just starting out and don't have much venture capital to begin testing with, then you *do* want to control your daily spending. But you do that by starting with a lower CPC at first, while leaving your daily budget safely higher so that your ads show for you around the clock.

But once you're profitable, you hardly need to worry about your daily budget, because for every click that you buy you get more money back. Again, it's all about your visitor value. If you know that your visitor value is $1.50 per click and you're aiming for a margin that's 30 percent above your Google costs, then you set your cost-per-click to no more than $1.15, and then leave it to run.

If it's profitable and *you know for a fact* that every single visitor spends an average of $1.50 with you, then you could theoretically set your daily budget limit way out of the ballpark and it wouldn't bankrupt you. Do be sensible about this, though. Of course you'll set your budget within a certain reasonable limit to prevent losses in early testing and also to prevent anomalous spending, such as sudden changes in a market or click fraud or unplanned errors with Google's system. But you be the judge of how much each click is worth to you, and control your spending by controlling your own cost-per-click.

MANAGE THE PERFECT GOOGLE CAMPAIGN

Picture for a moment the advantage that you could have if you knew all of this information:

- You start off with more keywords than your competitors have.
- You know what your prime hours are for visitors, and where the best ones come from.
- You know exactly which of your ads turns into the most sales.
- You know which keywords are selling the most, and which ones are selling the least.
- Every keyword has its own perfectly-tuned bid price.
- Your best ads are showing the most.
- You're bidding a separate amount, intelligently, for your content network traffic.
- You're managing your own spending budget wisely.
- You know at what page on your site visitors are leaving, and at what point they're being convinced to buy.

In the Google world (and the rest of the world, for that matter), the winner takes all. That last 1 percent of edge that this level of leverage will give you can mean the difference between you sitting at the top of a market, controlling it, or your competitor taking over. Which one will it be?

FAQ: Answers to All Your Frequently-Asked Questions about Google AdWords

Bryan and I have personally consulted with hundreds of people about their marketing projects and been inside of literally hundreds of Google AdWords accounts. The following questions are the most important and most common.

■ ■ ■

Better Clickthrough Rates, Better Prices

- What do you consider to be a good CTR?
- What's the best way to manage my daily, weekly, and monthly AdWords costs?
- Is there a difference between overall cost of advertising in the United Kingdom versus the United States or other countries?

Organizing Your Keywords and Keeping them Active

- How can I set up a new campaign so that my keywords get the highest possible CTRs?
- Should I have hundreds or even thousands of keywords in my ad groups?
- Why does Google say my keywords are "inactive"? What do I do about it?
- What is Google's secret keyword ranking formula?
- What's the best way to find the right keywords for my product without wasting money on trial and error?
- When should I use the "Peel & Stick" method on my keywords?

Where and When to Show Your Ads

- How do I split-test two ads?
- How many clicks does it take to declare a winner?
- What's the best position on the page for my ad to be in?
- Why aren't my ads being shown?
- How do I get my ads into the "preferred listings," those ultra-high-visibility, blue sponsored positions on the top left of Google's search results?
- I have two ads, but Google doesn't show them evenly. Why is this?
- If I'm split-testing two ads and I delete one of the two and write a new one, how should I compare the new ad's performance with the old one that's been running longer?

Better Landing Pages

- What's the best way to set up an opt-in landing page?
- What's the advantage of sending someone to an opt-in page vs. sending him directly to my sales letter?
- What if my site is simple e-commerce, where people quickly search, click, and buy?
- Can I have multiple different web sites selling the same product, all bidding on the same keywords and advertising on Google?

Testing Your Traffic and Getting It to Convert

- Do you recommend Google's conversion tracking?

- What tool do you recommend for split-testing landing pages?
- What do I do when I see that some of my keywords are converting to sales and some aren't?
- How do I track my sales back through Google if my customers buy from me in person or over the phone, rather than online?

Using Special Tools

- How reliable is Google's Traffic Estimator?
- What is Dynamic Keyword Insertion (DKI)?
- How do I insert " " quotes and [ ] brackets around my keywords automatically?

Pop-Ups

- Is there a way to deal with Google's policy of no pop-ups on the landing page?

Working in Specialized Markets

- How do I market a high-dollar item effectively on Google?
- My niche is specialized and I have found very few keywords that draw more than a few thousand requests per month. Is this still a good avenue for me?

Google's Regular Search Engine

- What's your number-one Search Engine Optimization (SEO) strategy?
- Does using Google AdWords improve your ranking on Google's regular organic search engine listings?

Google vs. Yahoo/Overture

- What's the biggest difference between Google AdWords and Yahoo/Overture?

Answers begin on the next page.

BETTER CLICKTHROUGH RATES, BETTER PRICES

Q: What do you consider to be a good CTR?

Traditionally, 1.0 percent is somewhat typical. However, there is no set number for this, *and every tenth of a point of improvement you get by strengthening your copy brings you more visitors.* Three percent is what I would consider to be a pretty respectable message-to-market match.

You can achieve CTRs of 10.0 percent or better when the text in the ad is a precise match to a *question* that the user types into a search engine. For example, note this ad:

Ethernet Basics Guide
Simple Tutorial on Ethernet, TCP/IP
5 Page Paper, Free Instant Download
www.xyzcompany.com

And note the one phrase in the keyword list that got the highest CTR by far:

Keyword	Clicks	Impressions	CTR
what is ethernet	5,314	32,481	16.3%

That 16.3 percent is one dang high CTR! And it wasn't hard to achieve at all.

So this suggests a strategy: What *ultra-specific questions* can you answer for your audience? Using those questions as key phrases will earn you excellent CTRs.

Q: What's the best way to manage my daily, weekly, and monthly AdWords costs?

Three simple principles for controlling your costs are:

1. Watch your daily budget, realizing that the daily amounts are very crude approximations.
2. Adjust your bids to keep yourself in the most cost-effective position on the search results page, which most of the time is not the top spot.
3. Constantly split-test so you can increase your CTR, and Google will give you better visibility without charging you more per click.

Q: Is there a difference between overall cost of advertising in the United Kingdom versus the United States or other countries?

Yes, in general there can be very significant differences in cost-per-click from one country to another, and also very big differences in the quality of the traffic, the kinds of things people buy, the prices people are willing to pay for those items, and the messages they respond to. You need to be very careful about the following points:

- Make absolutely sure you're not advertising in countries where prospects are unlikely to buy. You normally should not advertise in "all countries" unless you have a very specific reason to. A symptom of this is that Google tells you you're in position 4 but when you search for your own ad it shows in position 17. What's happening is you're #17 in the United States and #1 in Ethiopia. It's averaging #4, but not actually appearing in #4 in any country you could actually sell something to. Advertising in developing countries is risky. Large countries like India and China can bring you large amounts of poorly converting traffic if you're not careful.
- If you have a significant amount of traffic from multiple countries, you should build separate campaigns for each country. There's a lot of traffic available from the United Kingdom and the United States, for example, but buyers in the two countries can be quite different. Optimum ad copy, bid prices, and CTR's will be different for each country. Whether your product is priced in Pounds or Dollars, or whether you use English spelling ("realise") or American spelling ("realize") can make a significant difference.

ORGANIZING YOUR KEYWORDS AND KEEPING THEM ACTIVE

Q: How can I set up a new campaign so that my keywords get the highest possible CTRs?

First, follow our previous advice carefully, wherever it's humanly possible. *Only put keywords in an ad group that actually appear in the ad*, better still, in the ad's headline. If you've got keywords that don't match the ad, then take them out, stick them in a new ad group, and write a new ad that uses those specific keywords. Create as many different ad groups as you need to in order to make this work.

Second, at first only allow your ads to show on Google searches alone. Do this for the first few days or weeks until you've established that all your highest-traffic keywords are profitable.

When you click on "Edit Campaign Settings," you'll see that the "*Networks*" option lets you choose:

By default all of these boxes are checked. *We suggest that you uncheck all of them except for Google.* At the very least, uncheck the content network.

Why? Because in all likelihood the traffic that comes from content network sites (*New York Times*, Dictionary.com, and all of Google's AdSense users) will be of different quality than the traffic coming from just Google alone. In fact, the Google traffic could be better quality than even the search network traffic (AOL, Ask.com, EarthLink, etc.). So start with the most focused traffic that's most likely to turn into paying customers.

When you get that traffic profitable, turn on the other sources. In that case, your total volume of traffic may double or triple, or more, though it will be more of a challenge to turn into buyers. But why not start with traffic that's most likely to convert?

Q: Should I have hundreds or even thousands of keywords in my ad groups?

In a word, no. Now don't get me wrong. There's nothing bad about having a lot of keywords, *if* they're turning out a good CTR. But the rule of thumb that we've been telling you all along is this: if your keywords are in small, tightly-clustered groups that match their ads well and bring in plenty of clicks, then the more the merrier.

But you're just hurting yourself, and you're clogging up Google's already heavily loaded system if you throw 500 impossibly irrelevant search terms into one ad group and make one poor little ad carry the load. That's a sure-fire invitation to a very *low* CTR.

Also, you'll quickly discover the 80/20 rule at work in your keyword lists: more than 80 percent of your impressions and clicks will come from fewer than 20 percent of your keywords. Once you've identified your most productive keywords, then adding tons more keywords that stretch the impossible fringes of relevance to your ad groups will add miniscule benefits. It may even hurt you.

For advice on adding low-cost keywords that *are* relevant, check out Chapter 21 on turn-the-corner keywords.

Q: Why does Google say some of my keywords are "inactive"? What do I do about it?

Google gives your keywords two "status" levels: *active* and *inactive.* Google's algorithm calculates a minimum required bid for nearly every possible keyword under the sun, and if you won't pay Google's minimum required bid for a particular keyword, Google will simply put your keyword on "inactive" status and won't show your ad when folks search on that term. But as long as you agree to bid the required minimum amount or higher for a keyword, that keyword *will* trigger ads.

You have at least two options, not just one: 1) Bid what Google asks, or 2) tweak the copy of your Google ad to convince Google's computers that the ad is relevant. For option 2, the simplest way to get Google's computers to relax and require a lower bid from you is to take the keyword and stick it into the headline of your ad.

Q: What is Google's secret keyword ranking formula?

Google will never openly share with the world the exact formula that it uses to determine 1) your minimum bid price or 2) your ad's rank on the page. However, if we rank the key factors in terms of which ones make the biggest difference to your minimum bid, it breaks down roughly like this:

1. Historical keyword performance across Google
2. Keyword-to-adtext match
3. "Other" relevancy factors
4. Your CTR

Q: What's the best way to find the right keywords for my product without wasting money on trial and error?

Do your keyword research first on Overture. Check both the bid prices and the traffic quantity at http://inventory.overture.com. Bid prices are a *very crude indicator* of what traffic may be worth.

Note also that technical topics literally get ten times more searches on Google than Yahoo/Overture. So if you're doing keyword research on biology or something scientific or complex, you can be certain that Overture sites get far fewer searches than Google.

Also check out Google keyword tool, it's an excellent aid.

Use Google's traffic estimator. You can get estimates for keywords without having to actually add them to your list. And type in keywords on Google's regular search page to see how many other advertisers there are.

Wordtracker (www.wordtracker.info) is a powerful tool and serious AdWords marketers should have a subscription. Generally, you can get a very useful test of keywords and product concepts for a few hundred dollars.

Stephen Juth's AdWords Acceleration tool (www.AdwordsAcceleration.com) is great for finding under-served niches and keywords that have "slipped through the cracks" of other bidders.

Now *before* you spend any money, it would be a very good idea to see what other Google advertisers are doing. Some things to look at:

• How many advertisers are there? The number could be anywhere from one or two to several dozen. If there are fewer than eight bidders, you can get the bottom position for $0.05 or less.
• Tip: Pay attention to Google advertisers who split-test their ads. When you do a search on a keyword that you're researching, click the "Search" button

multiple times and you'll see that some ads change while others stay the same. The advertisers who split-test are almost *always* the sharpest pencils in the box.

• Go to Yahoo/Overture and find out what phrases are being bid on there.

Then when you *do* spend money, do one of the following two things:

1. Bid on lots of keywords and phrases, but keep your bid prices low. That will give you a lot of clicks on the cheaper words and phrases. Then track your results carefully.

2. Bid on a small number of words and phrases that are more popular and more expensive. They are somewhat more likely to have a higher conversion percentage, but be meticulous. Watch closely and track everything. If you're not getting opt-ins or sales, then try something else.

Q: When should I use the Peel & Stick method on my keywords?

You should use the Peel & Stick technique any time you have an important keyword that isn't performing at its absolute best. If there's a unique angle you know you can take with a particular keyword, or you have some keen insight into the psychology of that particular slice of the market, then pull that keyword out of its current ad group, and put it into a new ad group with a new ad to see if you can get it to perform better.

Wouldn't it be great if Google had a feature to do this for you automatically? Sadly, it doesn't. Manually delete the keyword and its closest variations from your old list, click on "Create a new ad group," and put in the new set of keywords with a new ad.

WHERE AND WHEN TO SHOW YOUR ADS

Q: How do I split-test two ads?

In each of your ad groups near the top of the page, Google displays the ad you're using. Right next to it is a small link that says "Create New Ad: Text Ad | Image Ad". Click on the link to write a second ad, and Google will automatically rotate it against the ad you've got now.

Let your traffic run for a while, and you'll be able to go back into your account and see at the bottom of the page how the two ads are performing against each other:

Want to Learn Chinese?
5 Crucial Principles You Must Know
To Master Chinese, and Fast
MasterChineseFaster.com
67 Clicks | 1.8% CTR

Want to Learn Chinese?
Everybody Else Sells Study Aids.
I Teach You a Whole-Life Strategy.
MasterChineseFaster.com
47 Clicks | 1.2% CTR

Q: How many clicks does it take to declare a winner?

Once each ad has 30 to 50 clicks or more, you can delete the loser and write another ad to test against the winner. If the difference in CTR is large, you don't need to wait that long; five or ten clicks will do.

If you want to know for sure whether the winner is really a winner, use the www.SplitTester.com tool. You can also go into Google's "Reports" page and run a report to find out how many conversions each ad results in.

Q: What's the best position on the page for my ad to be in?

This is something we talk about in more careful detail in our Ultra-Advanced Google AdWords Seminar (www.AdwordsBlackBelt.com). But here's a helpful thumbnail summary.

We've done the math on this as well as quite a bit of research. What we tend to find repeatedly is that you get the best ROI both away from the very top *and* away from the very bottom of the page.

The higher you are on a page, the more likely you are to get clicked on. But you're also more likely to get careless, click-happy people clicking on your ad and not buying. This is especially true in position one. And the very last position on a page might be easily ignored.

It ultimately depends on your market. In some markets, you'll want to be in top position as a means to become dominant. In other markets, you'd just be throwing money away.

Our Advanced Course (www.AdWordsBlackBelt.com) has more specific ROI charts and statistics on this question. Nevertheless, when all is said and done, the best answer is always: Test it and go with what works best for you in your own market.

Q: Why aren't my ads being shown?

Use Google's *Ads Diagnostic Tool* to find out. You can find this in "Campaign Management" on the green bar at the top of the page through the linked marked "Tools." Just enter a keyword from your list and Google will tell you why it might not appear:

Sometimes they'll give you multiple reasons. If this doesn't answer your question, call Google's customer service at 1-888-Google9.

Q: How do I get my ads into the "preferred listings"—those ultra-high-visibility, blue sponsored positions on the top left of Google's search results?

Our revered friends at *Planet Ocean* who specialize in search engine optimization offer these tips, which, if you've been paying attention to what we've been telling you throughout this book, should sound perfectly familiar:

1. You have to be bidding in fairly competitive, commercially oriented keyword categories. Not all keywords can get ads to show in those positions.
2. Your ad has to already be ranking near the top of the AdWords list for that keyword.
3. Your ad has to be earning a high enough CTR for Google to justify giving you the preferred positioning. The exact CTR you need? That's part of Google's secret formula. Savor the mystery!

Q: I have two ads, but Google doesn't show them evenly. Why is this?

Go back into your campaign view and click on "Edit Campaign Settings." *Uncheck* the box that says "Show better ads more often." Google should now show your ads roughly equally.

Q: If I'm split-testing two ads and I delete one of the two and write a new one, how should I compare the new ad's performance with the old one that's been running longer?

Keep a running log for your Google campaigns, such as in a Word document or text file, and record changes you make to your ads and the exact date that you made the change. That way you can go back into your Google account, set the date to when you submitted the new ad, and compare your performance just for the time period that both of your current ads have been running together.

BETTER LANDING PAGES

Q: What's the best way to set up an opt-in landing page?

What works best for us with opt-in pages is 100–300 words of copy, half of which is typically bullets. For a very clean, simple example, go to www.CyberWave.com.

This brief, minimum hype, straight-to-the-point approach seems to work very well. The worst opt-in success rate we've ever seen is about 4 percent. The best I've seen in a highly focused niche is over 50 percent, and 10 to 25 percent is very typical.

A few small changes in the right place can swing huge differences. We consulted with a customer of ours in the Netherlands and gave him a few helpful suggestions for how to structure his landing page, and his opt-in rate went from 3.5 to 10.7 percent, *literally overnight.*

Q: What's the advantage of sending someone to an opt-in page versus sending him directly to my sales letter?

Test it. It's hard now and getting harder to get a one-time impulse sale. Opt-ins can generate sales for you weeks, months, even years after the fact. And whereas 1 to 2 percent is often considered a good response to a sales letter, opt-in rates are usually ten times that.

A crude rule of thumb: If your product costs more than $50, think seriously about a multiple-step sales process. The more expensive your product is, the more steps you'll need.

Q: What if my site is simple e-commerce, where people quickly search, click, and buy?

Give people exactly what they want, when they want it.

Perry hopped online once in a hurry to find a set of quality steak knives for his wife's birthday. He needed them shipped before the following Monday. So he made the purchase, paid extra for fast shipping, and that was that.

Forcing customers to opt in on that type of site would be suicide. Make it as easy as possible for people to find you, get what they need, and check out.

Some simple rules of thumb are:

1. When you bid on a specific product keyword, send people straight to your page that sells that exact product.
2. Have your graphics and extraneous links take up as little space as possible on your page and show as much product as you can to convince visitors that you have what they need.
3. Have your checkout process take as few clicks and steps as possible. Clickbank does an excellent job of this for their clients and is a good model.
4. Always give visitors who aren't already in a hurry the option of signing up for free information, product offers, a catalog, a newsletter—anything to give you their contact information so you can stay in touch and sell to them again.

Q: Can I have multiple web sites selling the same product, all bidding on the same keywords and advertising on Google?

You can. But you'll just end up bidding against yourself.

But a legitimate argument for doing this would be if you had different versions of the same product, designed for different markets. Then you could put bids for both on the same keywords and get different slices of the same traffic. *That would be a good idea* and the best marketers do this a lot.

For example, if you were bidding on "flowers," you could have one site that sells fresh cut roses and another site that sells gift baskets. You might find that the two ads don't cannibalize each other. But even in this example you would need to be careful that you're filtering traffic to each ad using negative keywords, and not wasting impressions needlessly.

TESTING YOUR TRAFFIC AND GETTING IT TO CONVERT

Q: Do you recommend Google's conversion tracking?

Yes, by all means. It's far from flawless and not especially multidimensional. But it lets you track conversion all the way down to your individual keywords. That's something virtually no other program can do. We recommend using Google's tracker *plus* one or several other conversion trackers, which we talk about more below.

Q: What tool do you recommend for split-testing landing pages?

Hypertracker (www.Hypertracker.net) is a powerful tool for doing split-testing of multiple kinds—sales, opt-ins, landing page clickthroughs, and more. Hypertracker is an extremely capable tracking service that is surprisingly easy to understand and use.

In fact, we've put together a clear and helpful Hypertracker tutorial that shows you all the basics you need to know in order to set up and begin tracking landing pages, opt-ins, sales, and more. You can watch it for free in your favorite internet browser just by clicking on this link: http://video.hypertracker.net.

You can also use integrated services such as 1Shopping Cart (www.1Shop pingCartSystem.com). This is a full shopping cart service that lets you manage split-tests, autoresponders, affiliates, and more. To our knowledge, it's the easiest one-stop e-commerce solution available.

Q: What do I do when I see that some of my keywords are converting to sales and some aren't?

If you use Google's conversion tracking feature you will see that keywords differ wildly in their ability to convert to opt-ins or sales. Some keywords give you a cost-per-conversion of $1 and others can be as much as $500.

Rather than just deleting the poorly performing keywords, use the "Edit Keyword Settings" feature and check the box of the keywords that are not performing well. Rather than deleting them, just cut the bid prices *for those keywords only*. If you've been bidding $0.85 for the whole ad group and the keyphrase "Linux firewall" is converting poorly, cut the bid price to $0.20 or $0.30, and the conversion rate will probably go up. And the cost per acquisition will go way down.

In this example we've checked the boxes next to some of the creation/evolution keywords in our list, and we can edit their individual CPCs or URLs as we need to:

Why would your conversion rate go up? Because generally the harder people are willing to look to find you, the more likely they are to buy. *High bid positions get more low quality traffic; low bid positions get less traffic, but it's higher quality.* Sometimes the solution is to just be at position eight instead of position two, or to be on page two instead of page one.

Q: How do I track my sales back through Google if my customers buy from me in person or over the phone, rather than online?

You can use a 100-year-old technique from the print advertising world. For each keyword or ad group or campaign that you want to track, create a separate page on your web site with your phone number on it. With the number include a person's name or special extension that you can trace back to that ad group or keyword.

For example, "Call us at 1-888-518-8888 and ask for Rachel" or "Call us at 1-888-518-8888, extension 4431." Then have your receptionist record every time the caller asks for each code name or number. That way you'll know how well your ads or keywords are making your phone ring.

USING SPECIAL TOOLS

Q: How reliable is Google's Traffic Estimator?

The "Traffic Estimator" can be wildly inaccurate at times. You'll have to base your bids on past traffic and actual recorded campaign statistics, not on Google's estimates.

Q: What is Dynamic Keyword Insertion (DKI)?

If you want to spare yourself the time and effort of creating umpteen different ad groups for each of your keywords, you can use this feature. The keyword that people type in will automatically show up anywhere in your ad that you choose.

Here's how you set it up. For example, your keyword list includes the following terms:

adaptors
power adaptors
transformers

power supplies

power supply

then you would write up an ad like this:

{KeyWord:Adaptors} to Order

Quality Workmanship, Low Price

Free Shipping for $250 Orders or More

www.XYZ.com

That way any of the four terms in the keyword list above would show up in the headline, so that it would say "Transformers to Order" or "Power Supplies to Order" when people searched on them.

If people typed in keyword phrases that included the above keywords but were more than 25 characters total, then Google would just default and show the phrase "Adaptors to Order" in the headline.

This is a very effective tool under certain circumstances, and we discuss it in detail in our Ultra-Advanced Google AdWords Strategies Seminar (www.Ad WordsBlackBelt.com). There are some important guidelines to know concerning when and where to use the feature, what its limitations are, and precautions to take with it to avoid unwanted bad traffic and logistical nightmares.

Q: How do I insert " " quotes and [ ] brackets around my keywords automatically?

Our associate and fellow coach Howie Jacobson has a great little tool that does just that. It's called the Google Keyword Variant Generator, and it's available at www.TheAdTool.net.

POP-UPS

Q: Is there a way to deal with Google's policy of no pop-ups on the landing page?

There are several ways to deal with this. The easiest way is to make a different landing page specifically for your Google ads. Just change the name (e.g., /index-google.htm) and take out the pop-up scripts.

Pop-ups are often used to collect e-mail addresses for newsletters and the like. The larger question, though, is how to collect those e-mail addresses using a different method. One good technique is to use a "squeeze page" to offer a white paper or guide in exchange for an e-mail address, then show whatever you're trying to sell.

"Popovers" are those HTML pop-ups that you see now; they scroll down or slide over while you're viewing a page. Google usually lets them past its radar, and won't disapprove your landing page for having these unless an editor personally visits your site and manually checks for this. Be prepared in case Google's system disapproves your landing pages because of them.

WORKING IN SPECIALIZED MARKETS

Q: How do I market a high-dollar item effectively on Google?

Actually, many of the principles and techniques that apply to low-dollar, high-traffic B2C markets *do* also apply to high-dollar, low-traffic, suit-and-tie B2B markets. The important things to do are 1) know whether Google is the right tool for finding your customer, 2) separate *style* from *structure,* and 3) talk to your customers the same way they talk to each other and themselves.

Google is the ultimate instant gratification, get-it-now marketing machine. That means that in this industry your ideal customer may not be as likely to search on Google for your product. If this is the case, you'll need to find other venues to get your customer to find you.

Make yours an information site where you generate leads, not an e-commerce site. Trade your application and problem-solving information for prospects' contact information. Our favorite strategy for doing this is to offer reports, white papers, and troubleshooting guides—documents that help the customers solve problems. We've devoted an entire course to this subject at www.PerryMarshall.com/whitepapers.

Once you've collected the person's contact information, plug it into a highly targeted, content-rich autoresponder. Then use direct mail and the telephone to contact your prospects. Earn their trust by publishing quality information on a regular basis and "drip irrigating" them with follow-up mailings, your newsletter, opportunities to attend seminars, etc.

Please remember that you can use all of the tools that are common to online marketers—autoresponders, multiple web sites, search engine optimization, testing and tracking, streaming audio and video, Flash, live chat, and nearly every other tool used by mainstream marketers—even if you're in a highly specialized technical discipline. The only difference is how you write your copy.

Q: My niche is specialized, and I have found very few keywords that draw more than a few thousand requests per month. Is this still a good avenue for me?

That's perfectly fine. You can get very worthwhile results sometimes on keywords that get just a few searches a month. (I call them "nano-niches.") Many people will find that there's a finite amount of good traffic they can get on the internet, and that's it. Oftentimes there are a lot more customers in other, offline markets—trade shows, print media, direct mail, radio, TV, etc.

Sometimes it's less expensive to mail out postcards than to buy clicks.

I know one very successful internet marketer and self-publisher, doing over $1 million of business per year, who generates most of his traffic by advertising in magazines.

For information products, as opposed to physical products, traffic that comes through search engines is often *lower* quality than traffic that comes from offline sources.

There are some products for which Google is not a good traffic source.

There are some things Google AdWords isn't particularly good at doing. One such thing is attracting people who don't know they have a problem. If people don't know they have a problem, they'll never search for a solution on a search engine.

For example if you had a magic pill you could drop into your car's gas tank and double the gas mileage, it could change the world overnight. But you wouldn't want to introduce it to the world with Google AdWords because hardly anyone is searching for a pill like that. (Maybe no one is.) On the other hand a press conference would put the story of your pill on the front page of every newspaper in America.

Another example is toilet paper. I think it's safe to say that most of the world's six billion people use it, but only 13,442 searched Overture for it last month.

There are *many* advertising media available to you, from internet traffic to billboards to TV and radio to inserts in the Sunday newspaper. Each of these media has its own pros and cons. It's like that game Rock-Paper-Scissors. Sometimes

Google is the rock that smashes the scissors. Perhaps direct mail is the paper that covers the rock, and e-mail is the scissors that cuts the paper.

GOOGLE'S REGULAR SEARCH ENGINE

Q: What's your number-one Search Engine Optimization (SEO) strategy?

For a more complete treatment of Search Engine Optimization, see Chapter 24. But briefly, my strategy works like this:

1. Test a concept and tweak it using Google AdWords. Get it working smoothly and profitably there first.
2. Take it to Overture/Yahoo and possibly other paid search engines if you wish to buy more traffic. Use the copy that worked on Google as a starting point.
3. Be certain about your conversion rate and profitability on Google, then use that data to attract affiliates and buy traffic from nonsearch-engine searches.
4. After you've determined what keywords convert the best on Google, optimize (SEO) your web site for those keywords.
5. Similarly, build mini sites and doorway sites for those keywords.

This is not a book on Search Engine Optimization, but the most basic concept you should keep in mind is that once you've determined which keywords you really want rankings on, you need to pick your battles. Some keyword battles are *much* easier to win than others.

For example, if your company sells firewalls, you may find that the keyword "Linux firewall" is a good performer for you, but there are hundreds of other sites that are already optimized for this term and competing against you. This is a very hard battle to win. But maybe "corporate firewall" also performs well in your PPC campaigns, and there are a lot fewer sites optimized for that term. So you build your search engine optimization around "second tier" terms that get less traffic but are easier to win.

Q: Does using Google AdWords improve your ranking on Google's regular organic search engine listings?

No, it does not. Google maintains an editorial barrier between paid listings and free ones.

GOOGLE VS. YAHOO/OVERTURE

Q: What's the biggest difference between Google AdWords and Yahoo/Overture?

How do you need to approach Google AdWords differently than Overture? The short answer: They're completely different.

The key differences are:

- Overture, at the time of this writing, has a three- to seven-day waiting period and mandatory editorial review for each keyword and advertisement.
- Overture's maximum bid is a fixed number; Google discounts your bid down to $0.01 above the person below you, and usually you pay less than you bid.
- Overture does not reward you for good copy or penalize you for irrelevancy; its system is very straightforward. Google's is harder to master, but once you master it, it has tremendous advantages. (The Yahoo/Overture system will eventually be updated to reward high CTRs.)
- Google lets you change your ads instantaneously. That makes it the ultimate engine for testing ideas fast.

We're not gaga about Overture/Yahoo, but you could well double your traffic by advertising there. Also Yahoo is re-vamping their whole system so all of the above can change.

Google is constantly adjusting its system, and you can get more up to date information at www.perrymarshall.com/supplement.

Epiphany in Nairobi, Kenya

In September 2004, I took, literally, a trip around the world. I had a stop in Fiji, then to Coolum, Australia, where I spoke at the X10 Internet Marketing Seminar, then through Southeast Asia, the Middle East, and Africa: 17 days, 28,000 miles, and a fresh set of insights on our vast, yet very small planet earth.

■ ■ ■

Because my business runs on autopilot (thanks, in part, to the miracle of Google AdWords), I only spent about 30 minutes a day checking up on my business in cybercafés and had more money in the bank when I came home than when I left. That's a wonderful asset to have, but this chapter is about something bigger and more profound than that.

It's impossible to visit countries you've never been to before without having some kind of epiphany. Actually, I had a lot of epiphanies on this trip. But what's the *big* lesson?

I'm somewhere southwest of Nairobi, Kenya, visiting George and Jane Karanga, two very special people who run a foster program for AIDS orphans. I'm meeting a woman whose husband is dying of AIDS, he's down to 66 pounds; all kinds of kids who've lost both parents to HIV and now live with aunts, uncles, or grandparents; a seven-year-old boy who is deathly sick for lack of $1 for a bus ticket to go to a medical clinic; a woman who's eight years a paraplegic, living under a tin roof in a dark mud hut, her sole entertainment her radio, her cat, and her kind neighbors who look after her. Not a cheery scene.

But the epiphany occurs when I meet a fellow named Paul Mungai, who runs a cobbler shop. Paul, ironically, is crippled, but he knows how to make and fix shoes. And he knows how to run a business. He started with just $50 of seed money and now has by Kenyan standards a sound business. He's feeding his family, he's paying his rent, his kids have uniforms to wear to school, and everyone in his care has enough to live on.

We exchange a few words and share our mutual understanding: There is one and only one path out of poverty: *The one and only path out of poverty is entrepreneurship and business success.*

It ain't government. It's not social programs. It's not charity. It's not even jobs or technology. It's *entrepreneurship.*

The message was loud and clear:

> *What you and I do may be daring, crazy, irrational, and largely mis-understood. Condescending do-gooders may tell you you're greedy or too successful. Your brother-in-law may think you've got your head stuffed in a cloud. The government may think it has the right to confiscate your prof-its and give them to "education" or other well-intentioned social programs. You might cater to some strange market, doing something that most peo-ple consider frivolous.*

But the fact remains: What you and I do is profoundly important. You and I pave the road that leads from poverty to success. We create the ingenuity, jobs, and wealth that makes good medical care possible. We create a world that has enough to eat, a world where even welfare kids in housing projects get three square meals a day.

So don't ever apologize to anyone for doing what you do. If it wasn't for you, me, and the rest of us entrepreneurs, "they" would still be sleeping on dirt floors.

That conversation with Paul in Kenya sparkled with the mutual awareness of what I just described to you. And as George took me to see other recipients of Micro-Enterprise seed funding—a lady selling sardines and tomatoes on a nailed-together stand on the side of the road, several women selling fruits and vegetables in the local markets—I thought of the entrepreneurs I meet in the United States, Canada, and Australia. I thought of those rah-rah Amway rallies I was going to years ago, and the easily-exploited naiveté that's so characteristic of "the Biz Op" market as it's sometimes called.

Like it or not, it's that raw enthusiasm and independent spirit that drives the prosperity of the West. Where that drive, imagination, and ingenuity are lacking, people starve—literally.

So, yes, some business people are too greedy. Some entrepreneurs *don't* care about their fellow man. Some people do make their money by dishonest means. But remember, the character quotient is no better on the poor side of the fence.

If you're prospering by means of an honest enterprise, or if you're struggling to put one together, then I'm here to tell you that you are a hero. The bards and minstrels may not sing songs about you and your handsome face may never appear on *The Apprentice*, but what you do every day when you get out of bed is a worthwhile and indeed necessary thing. Don't ever forget it.

You can read the story of my entire 17-day trip, including strange tales of Oz, Singapore, Kuala Lumpur, and Dubai at www.perrymarshall.com/travelogue. And if you're interested in supporting Micro Enterprises in Africa, visit www.childrens relief.com.

About the Authors

PERRY MARSHALL

Perry Marshall is an author, speaker, and consultant in Chicago. He is known as "The Wizard of Google AdWords" and is one of the world's leading specialists on buying search engine traffic. Google advertisers who use his methods generate over half a billion clicks per month (conservative estimate). His company, Perry S. Marshall & Associates, consults with both online and brick-and-mortar companies on generating sales leads, and web traffic and getting maximum advertising results. Prior to his consulting career, he helped grow a tech business in Chicago from $200,000 to $4 million sales in four years, and sold it to a public company for $18 million.

He's spoken at conferences around the world and consulted in dozens of industries, from computer hardware and software to high-end consulting, from health and fitness to corporate finance.

BRYAN TODD

Bryan Todd is a writer and web traffic specialist in Lincoln, Nebraska. He's worked in both Europe and Asia and has spent most of his career teaching—from foreign language and world history to advanced testing methods for the internet. He has worked with clients in dozens of industries from health care and book publishing to manufacturing and computer software.

Index